Explore Kyoto through
the Artwork of a Japanese Pop Artist

Ki-Yan
ギャラリーを
めぐる

外国人が見つけた
KYOTO
グルメ & アート

Marta & Ki-Yan

ミシマ社

INTRODUCTION
まえがき

祇園祭を初めて観たときのことでした。八坂神社の前はとにかく人が多く、私は蒸し暑さに耐えられなくなって、目の前の店に逃げ込みました。店に入ったとたん急に私は暑さを忘れ、壁一面に広がるカラフルな別世界に包まれたのです。そこは、画家・木村英輝先生（Ki-Yan）の工房兼ショップ、「Ki-Yan Stuzio」でした。その瞬間から、私は Ki-Yan 作品の大ファンになりました。

その後、自著『魅惑の東欧・ポーランドインテリア＆雑貨めぐり』を知っていただいたことをきっかけに、今回この書籍のデザインを Ki-Yan から依頼されました。偶然 Ki-Yan 作品に出会い、惚れ込んだ私にとって、それは本当に嬉しい驚きでした。

本書では、Ki-Yan の拠点である京都に絞り、作品を紹介しています。また、Ki-Yan がよく使う色である赤・青・黄・銀・ワインレッドと様々な色を使ったマルチカラーの作品にならい、6つの章に分けて構成しました。

そして、ぜひ Ki-Yan 作品の魅力を世界に向かってご紹介したく、本書は日本語と英語のバイリンガル版です。文化の違いを配慮し、英文は対訳ではなく意訳にしました。Ki-Yan 作品の大胆で鮮やかな色彩、命を吹き込まれた動物や植物などのモチーフの魅力、日本の伝統美術を感じさせながらもポップでモダンな表現、そしてレストランから病院、警察にいたるまで誰もが見て楽しめる公共のスペースで展開されるアートに、私は魅了されます。高い美意識と素晴らしい技術、表現の普遍性を持った Ki-Yan 作品は世界中の人を惹きつけることでしょう。

この本を手にとって、ぜひ現地に足を運び、Ki-Yan 作品を体感してください。同時に、美味しいお料理やお買い物をお楽しみください！

マルタ・ヴァヴジニャク・イヂチ
Marta Wawrzyniak-Ijichi

It was my first Gion Festival . I was immersed in a crowd in front of Yasaka-jinja Shrine on an extremely hot and humid summer day. Feeling faint, I stumbled into the closest air-conditioned shop. To my surprise, the shop not only cooled me down, but also transported me to a fantastic world full of amazing paintings. I had discovered Ki-Yan Stuzio in Kyoto!

From that point on, I became a huge fan of the unique Japanese muralist Hideki Kimura (aka Ki-Yan). So much so that I purchased the 'Flying Elephants' silkscreen to celebrate my newly published guidebook introducing Polish interior design and products to a Japanese audience. I could have never guessed that the publication of that book would lead to a collaboration with Ki-Yan—the result of which you now hold in your hands!

Although Ki-Yan's paintings can be found throughout Japan, this book focuses on the artwork in his home base of Kyoto. Through a Japanese-English bilingual format, I wish to introduce Ki-Yan's artwork to the world. For English speakers not familiar with Japan, this book offers detailed explanations to help you to better understand the Japanese cultural context.

There are multiple reasons explaining my fascination with Ki-Yan's work. First, I love his use of bold and vibrant colour combinations, and his stylized fantastical motifs of animals and plants, which, though inspired by traditional Japanese art, are seamlessly transposed into a modern, pop-art setting. I also like the idea of art in public spaces — from restaurants, to hospitals and even police stations—which can be enjoyed by everyone. Given its universality and high aesthetic value, I believe Ki-Yan's artwork will be well received throughout the world.

This book is divided into six chapters according to Ki-Yan's favourite colours: red, blue, yellow, silver and wine red. The last chapter features multi-coloured works. The book has been designed to express the artworks' vibrant nature, not as two-dimensional wall decorations, but rather as intrinsic, lifelike parts of functional interiors.

Enjoy your trip through the colourful and exciting world of Ki-Yan!

Enjoy rocking paintings on the walls of Kyoto!

木村英輝　Ki-Yan

絵師。1942年大阪府生まれ。京都市立美術大学（現・市立芸術大学）図案科卒業。同大講師を務める。日本のロック黎明期に、日本初のロックフェスの開催、村八分のオーガナイザー、内田裕也とのワールド・ロックフェスなど数々のプロデュースを成し遂げ、伝説を残す。

還暦より絵師に。究極のアマチュアリズムを標榜し、「『ライブ』な街に絵を描きたい」と手がけた壁画は国内外で150ヵ所を超える。作品集に『生きる儘』『無我夢中』『LIVE』など。

HIDEKI KIMURA　Ki-Yan

Born in Osaka in 1942, painter Hideki Kimura (Ki-Yan) graduated with a degree in design from the Kyoto City University of Arts. Upon graduation, Ki-Yan first worked as a lecturer at his alma mater, then as a rock music producer. As an ambassador of rock and roll in Japan's early days of rock music, he produced the Japanese rock band Murahachibu, co-produced the world rock concert with Yūya Uchida, and organized many other legendary events, including Japan's first rock festival. Ki-Yan began his work as a mural artist at the age of sixty. Pursuing a form of ultimate amateurism, he has already painted more than 150 murals around Japan and abroad. His books include 'Ikiru Mama', 'Muga Muchū' and 'Live'.

Introduction まえがき 2

Chapter 1 6
RED

1. Tempura Kitamura 天魅羅きたむら 8
2. Hyakuren 百練 10
3. Hamamura 京都中華 ハマムラ 12
4. Hourandou Yasaka 峯嵐堂 八坂店 14
5. Hourandou Heian-jingū 峯嵐堂 平安神宮店 16
6. Miyabian 雅庵 18
7. Gyū Ōta 牛おおた 20
8. Zest ゼスト御池 22
9. Wine Kura Shiori Wine 蔵しおり 24
10. MK Bowl MK ボウル上賀茂 28

Chapter 2 30
BLUE

1. Gontaro 京都権太呂 本店 32
2. Kyoto City Zoo 京都市動物園 36
3. Kōtōen Yamashina 香東園やましな 38
4. SOU・SOU Zaifu SOU・SOU 在釜 40
5. Shōren-in Temple 青蓮院門跡 42
6. Yaoiso フルーツパーラーヤオイソ 44
7. Takii タキイ種苗株式会社 46
8. Clear リラクゼーションサロン Clear 48

Chapter 3 52
YELLOW

1. Goh-no Tora 五黄の寅 54
2. Takabashi Rāmen たかばしラーメン BiVi 二条店 56
3. CREVIA クレヴィア京都 四条後院通 58
4. Ki-Yan Stuzio 祇園本店・京都石段下店 60
5. Katsukura Kyoto Station
   かつくら 京都駅ビル The Cube 店 62
   Team Ki-Yan チーム キーヤン 64

Chapter 4 66
WINE red

1. CHIRIRI 京都つゆしゃぶ CHIRIRI 68
2. YAMASHITA 京・お漬物処 やました 70
3. Wabiya Korekidō 祇園花見小路本店 72
   侘家古暦堂
4. Restaurant VITRA レストランヴィトラ 74
5. Katsukura Higashinotōin
   かつくら 四条東洞院店 76
6. NOUVELLE VAGUE KYOTO
   ヌーベルバーグ KYOTO 80

Chapter 5 84
WHITE silver

1. Piito 匹十 (ピート) 86
2. Chōrakukan 長楽館 コーラル 88
3. TOKU 和牛焼肉 徳 92
4. Kyoto Hatoya 京湯元 ハトヤ瑞鳳閣 94
5. ADACHI 京の惣菜 あだち 98
6. Nakagyō Police Station 京都府警 中京警察署 102
7. Yume Kōbō Kyō 夢工房京 三年坂店 104
8. Toh-Lee からすま京都ホテル 中国料理 桃李 106
9. Taisushi 江戸前にぎり 鯛寿司 110
10. Kyoto Medical Center 京都医療センター 112

Chapter 6 114
MULTI colour

1. Doyanen どやねん 116
2. Kyoto Travelers Inn 京都トラベラーズ・イン 118
3. WAZAGU 京都国際工芸センター 120
4. eX cafe 京都嵐山本店 122
5. Takashimaya 京都タカシマヤ 126
6. Moriko ぎをん森幸 128
7. KOTOWA 京都八坂 132
8. GION WABIZA 祇園倭美坐 134
9. BAR HANARE 駒屋 花れ家 136
10. TANA-X 株式会社タナックス 138
11. Jūrokudai Gondayu 十六代権太夫 140
12. The Aglio Garden アーリオガーデン 144
13. Daichakai 祇園大茶會 146

COLLABORATIONS
1. SOU・SOU 150
2. ICHIZAWA SHINZABURŌ HANPU 152
3. EIRAKUYA 154
4. KOMARUYA SUMII 156
5. MIYAWAKI BAISEN-AN 158

Column 1 Gion Festival 祇園祭 50
Column 2 Rimpa 琳派 82
Column 3 Japanese Feng Shui 方位学 148

Epilogue あとがき 160
Info & Maps 161

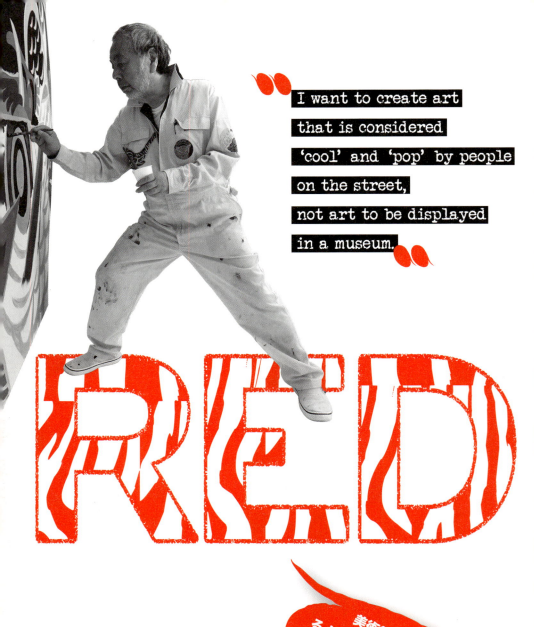

CHAPTER 1

1. Tempura Kitamura 天麩羅きたむら **8**
2. Hyakuren 百練 **10**
3. Hamamura 京都中華 ハマムラ **12**
4. Hourandou Yasaka 峯嵐堂 八坂店 **14**
5. Hourandou Heian-jingū 峯嵐堂 平安神宮店 **16**
6. Miyabian 雅庵 **18**
7. Gyū Ōta 牛おおた **20**
8. Zest ゼスト御池 **22**
9. Wine Kura Shiori Wine蔵しおり **24**
10. MK Bowl MKボウル上賀茂 **28**

1 TEMPURA KITAMURA
天麩羅きたむら

Blessings of Kyoto

目の前で海老や魚、旬の野菜がカラリと揚げられていく様子を、味わいの一つとして楽しめる「天麩羅きたむら」は、銅鍋をコの字に囲んだカウンター式のお店です。先斗町の路地奥にある隠れ家のような店へ案内してくれるのは、Ki-Yan手書きの看板と京野菜の絵。店内では、海老や魚が威勢よく飛び跳ねています。以前は画廊喫茶が入り、壁には絵画が掛けられていたんだそう。そんな場所に今、「額で飾られるような絵は描かない」というKi-Yanの壁画があるのは面白い偶然です。

The chef of Tempura Kitamura uses a copper pot at the counter to fry fresh seasonal vegetables, fish and shrimp right in front of guests. Located in Kyoto's atmospheric Pontochō Alley, this tempura restaurant is situated at the end of a narrow entrance that showcases Ki-Yan's iconic mural of Kyoto vegetables and a shop sign handwritten by the artist. Inside the small restaurant you will find another of Ki-Yan's paintings: giant shrimp and fish spiritedly jumping across the walls. In fact, before Tempura Kitamura occupied this space, it was home to a gallery-cafe. Therefore, you can still enjoy artwork here, but it is painted on the walls as Ki-Yan doesn't paint pictures to be framed.

How about some tempura?

1 京野菜の絵を目印に奥へ奥へ。**2** 海老、魚や野菜などが一品ずつ揚げられる。**3** 数寄屋風の店内で天麩羅の技を間近で堪能。**4** 最後は天茶漬け（or 天丼）で締め。

1 Use the *kyō-yasai* (Kyoto vegetables) paintings along the long, narrow entrance as a guide to get to Tempura Kitamura. **2** Fish, shrimp or vegetables—the chef fries each ingredient separately. **3** Enjoy the craftsmanship of tempura-making at the counter of the *sukiya-zukuri* (an architectural style based on tea house aesthetics) interior. **4** To finish, try *ten-chazuke* (mixed tempura on rice with green tea broth) or *tendon* (rice topped with tempura).

TEMPURA KITAMURA

map p165 - ⑮

京都市中京区先斗町
四条上ル 10M 西側

075-221-0011

11:00 ~ 15:00
17:00 ~ 22:00
closed Wednesday

3 min walk from Kawara-machi Station, Hankyū line

http://harukami.jp/kitamura

2 HYAKUREN

百練

Dancing Rose

繁華街・四条河原町にある路地を入った「裏寺」といわれる一角に、大衆食堂、居酒屋、鍋料理屋、酒場と幅広く楽しめる「百練」はあります。昼飲みができると観光客もわざわざ足を運ぶほど。ドアを開けるとすぐに急な階段が現れる2階の店は、カウンターとテーブル席があり、老若男女が好みのスタイルで賑わいます。「あえて店にミスマッチなものにした」とベニヤ板に華麗な赤いバラを描いたKi-Yan。ド派手な絵なのになぜか帰りになって気がつく人が多く、しばし立ちつくして眺めているそうです。

Popular among a wide range of customers, Hyakuren—known as a canteen, an *izakaya*-style pub, a *nabe* (hot-pot) restaurant or as just a bar—is located in a back alley of Kyoto's vibrant Shijō Kawaramachi area. As Hyakuren serves alcohol all day, it is a perfect spot to enjoy an early drink. Steep stairs lead you to the bar on the second floor, which features both table and counter seating. Ki-Yan intentionally painted the elegant roses on the rough plywood panels of the staircase to contrast to the pub's casual atmosphere. Although the gorgeous roses are so outstanding, apparently many of the customers notice them for the first time on their way back down the stairs…

1 初めて訪れる人はちょっと戸惑いながら上る階段。**2** ほわほわのだし巻卵。**3** 百練オーナーが錦市場に出す漬物「高倉屋」の盛り合わせもおすすめ。**4** Ki-Yanも大好きなステーキ定食。

1 Walk the narrow space between the 'Dancing Roses' and the vertically handwritten menus. **2** *Dashimaki tamago* (rolled omelette with *dashi* soup stock). **3** Assorted homemade pickles made by the Hyakuren's owner-chef—also sold at Takakuraya in Kyoto's Nishiki Market. **4** Hyakuren's steak set menu— one of Ki-Yan's favourites.

HYAKUREN

map p165 - ⑬

京都市中京区裏寺町通
四条上ル中之町 572
しのぶ会館 2F

075-213-2723

11:30 ~ 23:00
不定休

3 min walk from Kawara-machi Station, Hankyū line

www.hyakuren.com

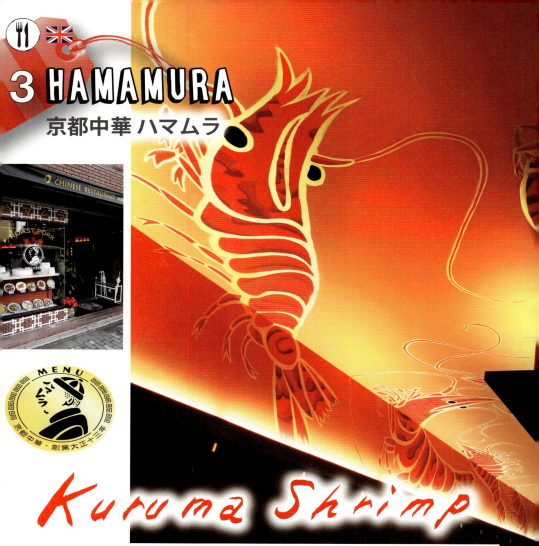

3 HAMAMURA
京都中華 ハマムラ

Kuruma Shrimp

1924年に創業し、京都の街で古くから愛されてきた「京都中華ハマムラ」。河原町三条下ルの店舗が閉店した際には多くの人が涙しましたが、2014年に満を持して移転オープン。京都の中華発祥の店として走り続けて90年、創業者の弟を祖父に持つ店主が腕を振るいます。新店舗での制作を依頼されたKi-Yanが「ここしかない」とひらめいて描いたのは天井。「食材で一番よく使う車海老を、カウンター席の上で弾ませたら面白い」と描き始めますが、上を向きながらの長い作業は大変だったようです。

Founded in 1924, Kyoto-Chūka Hamamura is one of Kyoto's oldest Chinese restaurants. While the closing of its popular Kawaramachi Sanjō-sagaru branch came as a shock to many regulars, the restaurant soon reopened at a new location. Family-run for over 90 years, this successful Chinese restaurant's current owner-chef is the grandchild of the founder's younger brother. Although painting on the ceiling is always a challenging task for the muralist, Ki-Yan wished to intrigue the guests by painting a mural of giant *kuruma-ebi* (Japanese tiger shrimp)—the most popular ingredient at this restaurant—directly above the counter seats.

1 京都中華を代表するさっぱり風味の酢豚。**2** 創業から人気の焼売。**3** オーブンでじっくりと焼かれた焼豚。**4** 胡麻団子はデザートに。

1 A light tasting version of *subuta* (sweet and sour pork)—a representative dish of kyoto-chūka (Kyoto style Chinese cuisine). **2** Popular dim sum style *shūmai* (pork dumplings). **3** Crispy *yakibuta* (roast pork). **4** Try *gomadango* (fried sweet sesame dumplings) for dessert.

HAMAMURA

map p166 - ⑫

京都市中京区丸太町通
釜座東入ル梅屋町 175-2
（府庁前）

075-221-4072

11:30 ~ 14:00
18:00 ~ 21:30 頃
closed Monday

5 min walk from Marutamachi Station, Karasuma subway line

http://hamamura.kyoto.jp

4 HOURANDOU YASAKA
峯嵐堂 八坂店

Heavenly beans and monkeys.

八坂の塔のすぐそばにある「峯嵐堂 八坂店」は、わらびもちと40種ほどの豆菓子がずらりと並ぶお店。近くの八坂庚申堂にちなんで決めたという申と、商品の豆が店内の壁面いっぱいに飛び交います。高いところが苦手なKi-Yanにとっては、緊張した現場の一つだとか。名物のわらびもちは自社特製で、前場信之社長が約2年かけて作った極上のきなこを、一番おいしく食べてもらうために作られたそう。店頭での「ぷるっ、とろっ」は素通りできない光景です。

Located just below Yasaka Pagoda, the Yasaka branch of Hourandou offers 40 kinds of *mamegashi* (beans snacks) as well as a selection of *warabi mochi* (a Japanese confection made from bracken starch). You may be surprised to see monkeys—a motif that comes from the neighbouring Yasaka Kōshindō Temple—and giant blue beans flying across the vermillion red walls and ceiling of the shop's traditional Japanese interior. Because of the high ceilings, this mural was one of Ki-Yan's most challenging pieces to complete! While taking in this spectacular work of art, try some of the famous soft, jelly-like *warabi mochi*. 'It took me two years to develop this *kinako* (roasted soybean flour) to match the taste of my homemade *warabi mochi* ', explains the shop's owner, Nobuyuki Maeba.

抹茶の味の黒豆
Dried kuromame matcha

丹波の黒豆
Dried kuromame
(black soybeans)
from Tamba

1 祇園・東山エリアの観光ついでに立ち寄れるロケーションにある。2 豆菓子は試食可。外国人には「さくさくわさび豆」が人気。3 店頭では職人が出来たてのわらびもちを切り分ける様子が見られる。4 出来たての箱詰めと、お土産用の真空パックタイプがある。

1 Take a brake at Hourandou Yasaka while sightseeing through the Higashiyama district. 2 Try the *saku-saku wasabi mame* (crunchy *wasabi* flavoured beans) — a favourite among foreign guests! 3 Come to the shop to see how *warabi mochi* is made! 4 Freshly packed *warabi mochi*.

HOURANDOU YASAKA

map p166 -⑱

京都市東山区八坂通下
河原町東入ル金園町 388-10

075-525-0507

10:00 ~ 18:30
年中無休

5 min walk from Kiyomizu-michi bus stop, bus 206 and 100 from Kyoto Station

http://hourandou.net

5 HOURANDOU HEIAN-JINGU

峯嵐堂　平安神宮店

Heian Shisin & Beans

八坂店と同じく、わらびもちと豆菓子を提供する「峯嵐堂　平安神宮店」。こちらでは店内で出来たてのわらびもちがいただけます。京都の料亭などに豆や昆布、海苔など乾物を卸す「峯嵐堂」が、とくに大豆にこだわり、絶妙な加工ブレンドから作った極上のきなこ。これをおいしく食べてほしいと作ったわらびもちと、40種以上の豆菓子が並びます。壁には平安神宮にちなんで四方を護る四神、青龍、朱雀、白虎、玄武が。お土産用の真空パックはKi-Yanの提案で、4つセットの四神デザインになったそうです。

Hourandou Heian-jingū offers the same product range as the company's Yasaka branch—its famous *warabi mochi* (a Japanese confection made from bracken starch) and 40 kinds of *mamegashi* (bean snacks). The difference is that here you can sit down and enjoy a beautiful set of freshly made *warabi mochi* and *matcha*! Hourandou supplies Kyoto restaurants with soybeans, *kombu* and other dried ingredients, and is especially proud of its high-quality *kinako* (roasted soybean flour) developed to perfectly match the taste of its homemade *warabi mochi*. The motifs of the 'Four Deities' pained on the café's walls are connected to the neighbouring Heian-jingū Shrine and represent the four cardinal directions: tiger for the West, peacock for the South, turtle for the North, and carp for the East.

1 店頭で切り分けられるわらびもち。**2** きなこ味や抹茶味、竹炭入りの黒いわらびもちに黒胡麻をかけた3種を一度に味わえる「とろけるわらびもち（おうすつき）」。**3** シンプルに味わえる「おうすとわらびもち」。**4** 四神デザインの、日持ちタイプのわらびもち。

1 Take a look through the café's window to see how *warabi mochi* is made! **2** Try the Melting *warabi mochi* set served with *matcha* and three flavours of soft *warabi mochi*—*kinako*, *matcha* and charcoal topped with black sesame. **3** A simple set of matcha and *warabi mochi*. **4** Thanks to Ki-Yan's suggestion, the 'Four Deities' can be found on *warabi mochi* gift boxes—a different motif for each flavour!

HOURANDOU HEIAN-JINGU

map p167 -③

京都市左京区岡崎円勝寺町
140 ポルト・ド岡崎 105

075-741-7636

10:00 ~ 18:00
年中無休
5 min walk from Higashiyama Station, Tōzai subway line

http://hourandou.net

6 MIYABIAN
雅庵

Lucky Bamboo

おいしい京野菜としゃぶしゃぶの店「雅庵」の階段を彩る、赤と黒の「竹」。制作に入ったその場で急遽変更されたモチーフで、すぐに構図を練り直して一気に描き上げられた作品です。階段下から眺める竹にはそんな当時の勢いが今も伝わるのか、訪れた人の視線を集めます。しゃぶしゃぶ、すき焼き、豚しゃぶなど各コース食べ放題が人気。外国人客の来店も多く、最初は「おかわり自由」のコースにびっくりするとか。一つだけある茶室風の個室はぜひカップルで！

Specializing in *kyō-yasai* (Kyoto vegetables) and *shabu-shabu*, Miyabian features an elegant staircase lined with red and black bamboo. Just after Ki-Yan began painting, he spontaneously deviated from his initial plans and completed this mural in a very short amount of time. Before walking up to the second floor to enjoy your *shabu-shabu*, *sukiyaki* or *buta-shabu*, take a minute to admire the impressive 'Lucky Bamboo' from the best vantage point: the bottom of the stairs. Don't miss out on Miyabian's all-you-can-eat courses and free refill service. The restaurant also has one private tea house-style room that is very popular among couples.

1 賑やかな通りから一歩入ると、雅な京情緒ただよう世界が広がる。2 若鶏の唐揚チリソースがけ。3 生麩盛り合せ。4 霜降り国産牛すきしゃぶ食べ放題。

1 Step back from the bustling street and find serenity in Miyabian's Japanese garden. **2** A side dish of *wakadori karaage* (fried chicken) topped with chilli sauce. **3** Assorted *namafu* (wheat gluten) come in many shapes and colours, including the shape of Japanese maple leaves. **4** An all-you-can-eat course of *shimofuri* (marbled) wagyu beef *shabu*.

MIYABIAN

map p164 - (4)

京都市中京区六角通富小路
西入ル大黒町71 イーグル
コート京都六角雅心庵1F

075-253-0291

17:00 ~ 23:00
無休(大晦日・元旦除く)

10 min walk from Karasuma-Oike Station or Shijō Station, Karasuma subway line

www.k-company.net/miyabian

7 GYU OTA
牛おおた

Red Tiger

上質の肉をじっくりと味わいたい人が通う焼肉店。国産和牛は産地にこだわらず、その日の最高のものを仕入れるスタイルがうまさの秘訣です。おすすめはミスジとサンカク。またテール蒸しやハルサメなど韓国惣菜のサイドメニューも見逃せません。焼肉→韓国→トラという連想から、「食べ物屋にはあたたかさがないとうまい料理が味わえない」という考えで描かれた赤いトラ。「枠からはみ出るほうがKi-Yanらしい」という友人の一言をうけ、尻尾は後から柱を超えて描き延ばしたそうです。

If you are looking for fresh and high quality meat in Kyoto, opt for the *yakiniku* (authentic Japanese BBQ) restaurant Gyū Ōta. The restaurant's superior flavours come from its choice of quality meat—the best Japanese wagyu beef of the day, regardless of region of origin. And don't forget to try the *misuji* (oyster blade) and *sankaku* (chuck ribs), both highly recommended by the owners. Along with carefully selected meats, the restaurant also offers various Korean side dishes including steamed oxtail and *harusame* noodle salad. The idea of the red tiger painting for this *yakiniku* restaurant comes from a popular association in Japan among grilled meat, Korea and tigers, as well as Ki-Yan's desire to paint the tiger in warm colours in order to enhance guests' dining experience. Following a friend's suggestion, the artist later repainted the tiger's tail over the corner pillar.

1 1階はカウンターとテーブル席。赤いトラは2階のVIPルーム。**2**「てっちゃん」。**3** 人気の「上タン塩焼き」。**4** おすすめの「ミスジ」は売り切れゴメン。

1 Counter and table seating on the first floor. The 'Red Tiger' can be found in the private room upstairs. **2** *Tetchan* (intestine). **3** The popular *jōtan-shioyaki* (grilled salted beef tongue). **4** Try the popular *misuji* if it is not already sold out!

GYU OTA

map p166 - ㉕

京都市左京区浄土寺
真如町164-9

075-751-7888

17:00 ~ 23:00
closed Monday

0 min walk from Shinnyodō-mae bus stop, bus 5 from Kyoto Station

www.gyu-ohta.com

8 ZEST ゼスト御池

map p165-②

Carp is dragon in heaven

9 WINE KURA SHIORI
Wine 蔵しおり

The Kings of beasts & flowers

「百獣の王と百花の王」をテーマにした、迫力満点のライオンと牡丹が出迎えてくれる「Wine蔵しおり」は、約90種のワインと創作料理が気楽に楽しめるダイニングバー。京町家の趣きをそのままに、掘りごたつ式の個室やテーブル、カウンターなど様々なスタイルで過ごすことができます。壁の角から見つめるライオンや天井まで広がる牡丹など、枠にとらわれないKi-Yanスタイルがあちこちに。2階の白い箱庭にあるブドウが眺められる席は絶対おすすめ。心地よいほろ酔いを誘います。

Home to Ki-Yan's dynamic mural 'The Kings of Beasts and Flowers', Wine Kura Shiori is a dining bar serving over 90 types of wine alongside inventive international and Japanese inspired dishes. Located in a renovated *kyō-machiya* (traditional Kyoto townhouse), the bar provides a variety of seating styles, including the popular *horigotatsu* seating style (seating at a table over a sunken floor) in the private room. Ki-Yan's paintings of red lions and peonies that dominate the staircase walls represent the artist's signature style of 'painting without boundaries'. Don't forget to check out Ki-Yan's 'Grape Terrace' on the second floor—a blue mural on the white walls surrounding a miniature Japanese rock garden.

1 迫力満点の赤いライオンと牡丹が2階へとご案内。 **2** 天使の海老とアスパラの香草グラチネ。 **3** 名物石焼きトマトリゾット。

1 Follow the red lions and peonies to the second floor. **2** Angel shrimp gratin with asparagus and herbs. **3** *Ishiyaki* stone-grilled tomato risotto, a specialty of the restaurant.

1 京町家の中にブドウ畑が広がる不思議な空間。
2 カキのアヒージョ。 3 ワインのメニューに迷ったときは、スタッフに相談！ 4 サーモンとアボカドの生湯葉ロール。 5 彩り鮮魚のカルパッチョ。
1 Experience the change in colour—from the fiery reds on the stairs, to the cool ultramarine blues on the second floor. 2 Enjoy the garlic aromas of the hot oyster ajillo. 3 Choose from a rich selection of wines. 4 Salmon and avocado *yuba* (tofu skin) rolls. 5 Colourful fresh fish Carpaccio.

WINE KURA SHIORI

map p167 - ⑥

京都市下京区七条通新町
東入ル西境町158

075-365-1377

17:00 ~ 24:00
無休

5 min walk from Kyoto Station

www.shioriya.com

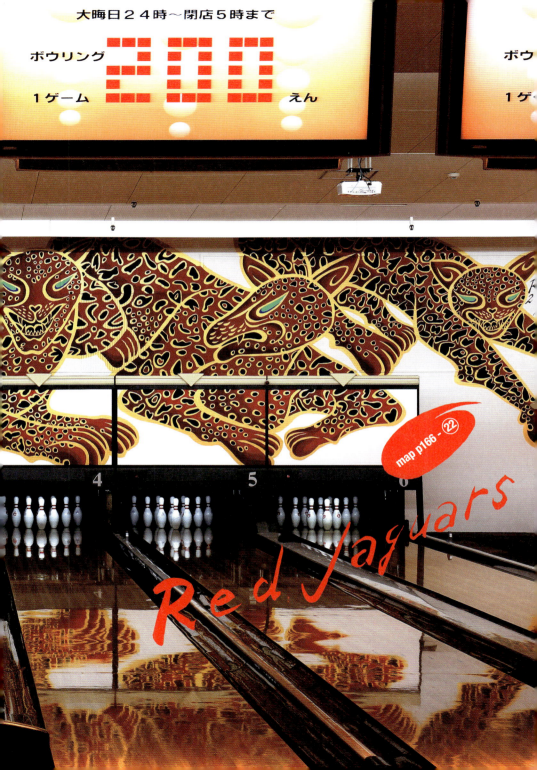

何時までも、素人でいたい。素人裸足、究極のアマチュアを目指すだけ。

BLUE

"I don't want to be
a professional painter.
I am simply pursuing
a form of
ultimate amateurism."

CHAPTER 2

1. Gontaro 京都権太呂 本店 **32**
2. Kyoto City Zoo 京都市動物園 **36**
3. Kōtōen Yamashina 香東園 やましな **38**
4. SOU・SOU Zaifu SOU・SOU 在釜 **40**
5. Shōren-in Temple 青蓮院門跡 **42**
6. Yaoiso フルーツパーラーヤオイソ **44**
7. Takii タキイ種苗株式会社 **46**
8. Clear リラクゼーションサロン Clear **48**

Column 1 Gion Festival 祇園祭 **50**

1 GONTARO
京都権太呂 本店

毎朝、昆布やサバ節など選び抜かれた素材で丁寧に引いた出汁が自慢。その旨味は「名物権太呂なべ」をはじめ、蕎麦やうどんで楽しむことができます。京都の繁華街にある本店ビルは和風の佇まい。のれんをくぐれば打ち水された石畳が奥へ続き、数寄屋造りの落ち着きのある店内は椅子席から座敷まで揃います。3階に広がる蕎麦の花は、権太呂所有の蕎麦畑でスケッチされたもの。花の中のカマキリは、Ki-Yanがこの壁画の構想を練っていたとき、偶然自宅に飛び込んできた珍客。そのままモデル採用?!となりました。

Gontaro prides itself in its *dashi*—a homemade soup stock made of carefully selected *kombu* and mackerel flakes prepared freshly every morning. Enjoy the *umami* taste of this *dashi* in the Famous Gontaro Hot Pot, *udon* noodle soup or *soba* buckwheat noodle soup. This main branch of Gontaro is located in Kyoto's busy shopping area in a modern building with an authentic *sukiya-zukuri* (an architectural style based on tea house aesthetics) style interior. The restaurant features both table seating as well as Japanese style tatami rooms. You can find Ki-Yan's paintings of buckwheat flowers on the walls and the sliding doors on the third floor. These paintings are based on sketches Ki-Yan drew while in Gontaro's own buckwheat fields. You can also find the motif of a praying mantis sitting on a buckwheat flower. While thinking about the composition of the paintings for Gontaro, a praying mantis jumped into Ki-Yan's house, and he spontaneously decided to feature the insect as well.

1 料理のメニューにも蕎麦の花。**2**「鴨なんばんそば」はやわらかい鴨肉とネギが絶妙。**3** サクサク感が人気の「天ざるそば」。

1 Ki-Yan's buckwheat flowers decorating Gontaro's menu. **2** *Kamo-nanban soba*—buckwheat noodles with soft duck meat and *negi* (spring onion). **3** The crispy *Tenzaru soba* set—cold buckwheat noodles with hot tempura and dipping sauce.

人気の天ざるそば！
Try our
Tenzaru soba set！

1 絵のある3階座敷からは東山が望める。
2 絣の前垂れに赤いたすきのスタッフが京ことばでお出迎え。3 ぜひ食べてほしいとろろの「自家製抹茶わらび餅」。

1 Indoor Japanese style garden with a view on Higashiyama on the third floor just opposite the large tatami room with Ki-Yan's paintings. **2** A waitress wearing a traditional indigo-dyed *kasuri* (splash pattern) apron welcomes guests in Kyoto dialect. **3** For dessert, try the homemade *matcha warabi mochi* (green tea flavoured Japanese confection made from bracken starch).

Have a great time at Gontaro!

2

3

GONTARO

map p164 - ⑩
京都市中京区麩屋町通
四条上ル

075-221-5810

11:00 ~ 21:00
closed Wednesday

5 min walk from Shijō Station,
Karasuma subway line

http://gontaro.co.jp

2 KYOTO CITY ZOO
京都市動物園

香東園やましな

3 KOTOEN YAMASHINA

map p166 - 28

38

4 SOU·SOU ZAIFU
SOU・SOU 在釜

Water Land.

在釜は、和のしつらいに京都のブランド「SOU・SOU」のスタイルを取り入れた、気軽に茶の湯の雰囲気を楽しめるカジュアルなお茶席です。「Water Land」は2009年に店内の壁に描かれましたが、改装で天井を取り払うことになり、現在では屋外の壁画として昼夜異なった表情を見せています。

睡蓮や蓮にはじまる、水辺の世界を描いたKi-Yan作品は、青蓮院門跡の襖絵から始まりましたが、「SOU・SOU」とコラボした足袋などの商品でも身近に楽しむことができます。

SOU・SOU Zaifu is a spot in Kyoto where you can experience the traditional atmosphere of *chanoyu* (Japanese tea ceremony) in a contemporary setting. Zaifu's modern Japanese interior features fabric products by SOU・SOU—a Kyoto-based brand producing unique fashion pieces and footwear. Ki-Yan's mural 'Water Land' was originally painted in 2009 for SOU・SOU's men's apparel store Kei-i, but became part of the patio leading to Zaifu following renovations and the removal of the ceiling. Originally appearing on the *fusuma* sliding doors in Shōren-in Temple, these water based motifs— including motifs of lotus flowers, water lilies and frogs — can also be found on a number of SOU・SOU products made in collaboration with Ki-Yan, such as the brand's signature *jika-tabi* (split-toe shoes).

1 地下1階の「Water Land」。一緒に水の世界にもぐって眺めるようで面白い。
2 隠れ家的な雰囲気にワクワク。**3** 二十四節気と七十二候が書かれた壁面もチェック。**4** 珈琲は下鴨の「カフェ・ヴェルディ」によるSOU・SOUオリジナルブレンド。**5**「亀屋良長」とコラボした和菓子は月替わり。毎月通うファンも多い。

1 A mixture of Ki-Yan's fantasy world and reality—green plants on the patio reflecting in the mirror-like surface of the 'Water Land' painting, a part of the curved wall mural. **2** Welcome to the 'Way of Tea' space. **3** Check out the East Asian calendar system decorating Zaifu's interior. The staff stylishly dresses in SOU・SOU attire. **4** Enjoy the unique coffee making process—prepared in the same traditional way as *matcha*—made from a SOU・SOU original blend created by caffe Verdi in Shimogamo, Kyoto. **5** *Wagashi* Japanese sweets change monthly and are made in collaboration with Kyoto's traditional confectionary shop, Kameya Yoshinaga.

SOU・SOU ZAIFU

map p164 -⑪

京都市中京区新京極通
四条上ル二筋目東入ル
二軒目 P-91ビル B1F

075-212-0604

12:00～20:00
無休

5 min walk from Kawara-machi Station, Hankyū line

www.sousou.co.jp

青蓮院門跡

5 SHOREN-IN TEMPLE

map p167 - 5

6 YAOISO
フルーツパーラーヤオイソ

「もっとフルーツを食べてほしい」と40年以上も前から作られている「フルーツパーラーヤオイソ」の看板メニューは、フルーツサンド。4軒隣りにある、創業120年の本店ヤオイソで吟味されたたっぷりのフルーツを特製のクリームと一緒に食パンではさんだ、切り口も美しいサンドイッチです。Ki-Yanは「自然主義的な印象になるから」と緑色は使ずに、フルーツサンドに使われるメロンやモモ、サクランボなどを鮮やかなウルトラマリンで躍らせました。とくに、メロンの絵が見られるのは現在ここだけです。

Fruit sando, the main menu item at Fruit Parlour Yaoiso, has been served for over 40 years as a way to encourage people to eat more fruit. Only high quality fruit sold in the Yaoiso main store—in operation since 1869 and located just four doors down from the parlour—is used in these tasty sandwiches. Coming in many varieties, the *fruit sando* consists of beautiful cuts of fresh fruit—from strawberry to kiwi—and plenty of soft cream sandwiched between two slices of fluffy, white bread. On the parlour's walls, Ki-Yan combined colours of vivid ultramarine blue to paint the 'Waltzing Fruits' motifs of melons, peaches, cherries and more. 'I purposely avoided using green, as it could create too much of a "naturalistic" impression', explains the artist.

1 スペシャルサンドとミックスジュースのセット。**2** イチゴの季節にはイチゴサンドが登場。**3** 旬のフルーツでミックスされるから味は微妙に変化。

1 Special *fruit sando* with mixed juice set. **2** Enjoy a strawberry sandwich during strawberry season! **3** Mixed fruit juice. The flavour will differ slightly depending on the season.

YAOISO

map p166 - ⑰

京都市下京区四条大宮
東入ル立中町496

075-841-0353

9:30 ~ 17:00
無休(年末年始、X'mas を除く)

1 min walk from Ōmiya Station, Hankyū line or Shijō-ōmiya Station, Keifuku (Randen) line

http://yaoiso.com

タキイ種苗株式会社

map p167 - ⑧

Lively Earth 47

8 CLEAR
リラクゼーションサロン Clear

Rosellas & Eucalyptus

オーストラリアで古くから、スキンケアや風邪、切り傷などの治療薬として手軽に使われてきたアロマオイル。本場の地でアロマセラピストとして勤務した平川真理子さんは、帰国後、リゾートホテルのサロン勤務を経て「Clear」を立ち上げました。Ki-Yanに壁画を描いてもらうのが念願だったため、新築のサロンルームには最初から白の空間を準備。Ki-Yanにとって初となるモチーフであるインコとユーカリが縦横にのびのびと描かれ、みんなを元気で包んでいます。

Essential oils have been used in Australia for many years for a wide variety of wellness applications from skin care to healing the common cold. Having worked as an aromatherapist in Australia and in resort hotel beauty salons in Japan, Mariko Hirakawa has opened the salon Clear with the intention of offering personalized, individual care to each and every customer. Having left white space on her walls in hope that Ki-Yan would someday paint a mural, Mariko's wish finally came true. The parrots and eucalyptus—Ki-Yan's new motifs painted not only on the walls but also on the window screen—energize everyone who enters the room.

1 オーストラリアのアロマオイルのトップブランド、AUROMA社の製品を使用。 **2** 薄暗い空間に青が浮かんで幻想的。 **3** 「Angels Oracle Cards」はポジティブになれると好評。 **4** 「サロンのオープン時にはぜひ絵を描いてほしかった」という真理子さんとご家族。

1 AUROMA, Australia's leading supplier of essential oils. **2** The shiny ultramarine blue provides a dreamy feeling during treatment. **3** Angels Oracle Cards used during treatment. **4** Mariko with her family.

CLEAR

場所は予約時にご案内
（嵯峨野・亀岡2カ所にて）

by appointment only
price available on request

mobile:
080-1475-5202

e-mail:
ko.a.la.12.25@docomo.ne.jp

GION FESTIVAL
祇園祭

　四方を山に囲まれた盆地の平安京は、夏は蒸し暑く、冬は底冷えする厳しい自然気象に悩まされてきた。特に夏は疫病でも発生したら都が滅びかねないほどの打撃を受ける。そこで疫病退散を祈願し、矛を立て、町衆の祭り「祇園祭」が始まった。ただ願うだけではなく、疫病への抵抗力をつけるため滋養のある食べ物を食する"しきたり"を祭りに結びつけたのだ。祇園祭を別称"鱧祭"と呼び、鱧料理で滋養を補足するようになった。

　海から遠い京の都は、町衆の智恵で魚もうまく食生活に取り入れた。骨切りの鱧、ひと塩の鯖とグジ（甘鯛）。そして鴨川などで獲れる鮎、ゴリ、鯉、うなぎなどの川魚料理。さらに賀茂なす、万願寺とうがらし、桂うりなど夏を元気に越すための食材を、私は提灯に描くことで、もう一つの祇園祭を祈ることにした。

Kyoto, a city surrounded by mountains and shaped like a basin, suffers from harsh climatic conditions including very hot and humid summers, and cold winters that can chill you to the bone. Historically, given the summer heat, plagues could quickly spread and destroy the city. Therefore, the merchants' festival, Gion Festival, began with the ritual of setting up a pike and praying to calm the outbreak of disease. The people of Kyoto not only prayed, but also began the custom of consuming highly nutritious foods to increase their resistance to disease. Gion Festival was also called Hamo Festival because *hamo* (pike conger eel) was considered to be very nutritious.

Although Kyoto is located far from the sea, the merchants of Kyoto introduced fish into the local diet. There are many fish dishes in Kyoto, which use *hamo*, lightly salted mackerel, *guji* (horse-head fish), *ayu* caught in the Kamo River, *gori*, carp, eel and other fresh water fish. Moreover, there are many seasonal vegetables such as *kamonasu* (a round-shaped eggplant), *manganji* pepper or *katsura* gourd – all which helped to keep people healthy during the summer. So, by painting these motifs on paper lanterns, I tried to contribute to Gion Festival in my own way.

> 能書きをさけて、勢いと切れ味を描きたいから、画題に 修飾語をさけ、動詞を使う。

YELLOW

" I avoid boasting about my work, but am eager to convey a sense of vigour and sharpness about my paintings, so I use verbs rather than adjectives in my titles. "

CHAPTER 3

1. Goh-no Tora 五黄の寅 **54**
2. Takabashi Rāmen たかばしラーメン BiVi 二条店 **56**
3. CREVIA クレヴィア京都 四条後院通 **58**
4. Ki-Yan Stuzio 祇園本店・祇園石段下店 **60**
5. Katsukura Kyoto Station かつくら 京都駅ビル The Cube 店 **62**

Team Ki-Yan チーム キーヤン **64**

1 GOH-NO TORA
五黄の寅

メインとなる京都丹波の京鴨と朝引きの新鮮な紀州梅鶏の炭火焼料理のほか、おばんざいなど創作料理が得意。京都発のブランド「SOU・SOU」とのコラボレーションによるファブリックと和のテイストに包まれた店内は、気持ちが落ち着く空間です。

基本的に、モチーフそのものの色は使わないのが常であるKi-Yanですが、こちらはストレートに店名から「Five Yellow Tiger」という作品が完成。黄色を主とする5色で描かれたトラは、1匹でも迫力満点です。

Goh-no Tora serves *obanzai* style Kyoto cuisine while also specializing in inventive menu items such as charcoal grilled duck from Kyoto's Tamba region, or *Kishuumedori*—an original brand of chicken from Wakayama raised on *ume* plum vinegar. The name of the restaurant ('five yellow tigers') comes from the chef's astrological data: the combination of the year of the Tiger, the number five, the colour yellow and the Earth Star according to the Nine Star Ki form of astrology. In line with the name of the restaurant, Ki-Yan, who usually doesn't paint his subjects with realistic colours, decided to use yellow for the tiger and expressed the number '5' by using five colours: yellow, red, black, orange and gold.

1 和紙の灯りが安らぐカウンター。2 季節のちょこっとパフェ。3 寅の炭火焼き野菜三種盛り。4 五黄のサラダ。5 店内のファブリックは「SOU・SOU」プロデュース。

1 Counter seats at the bar facing a wall made of translucent Japanese *washi* paper. 2 A seasonal piccolo parfait. 3 Three kinds of charcoal grilled vegetables. 4 Goh-no Tora salad, a house special. 5 SOU・SOU designed coaster. SOU・SOU fabrics are also used on cushions, giving a modern Japanese touch to the restaurant's interior.

GOH-NO TORA

map p164 - ㉓

京都市下京区四条町369

075-343-7309

18:00 ～ 25:00
closed Tuesday

3 min walk from Shijō Station, Karasuma subway line or Karasuma Station, Hankyū line

2 TAKABASHI RAMEN
たかばしラーメン　BiVi 二条店

醤油ベースの豚骨スープにストレート麺、京都を代表するラーメン屋。"安い、おいしい、早い"に"元気"をプラスした店内はいつも活気に溢れています。開店から半世紀を経ても変わらぬ老舗の味には、昔からのファンもたくさん。さらには店舗リニューアルの際に登場した大輪のヒマワリとおしゃれな内装に「女性やシニアも入りやすい」と、より幅広い客層が並ぶようになりました。メニューもスタッフも常に革新的なお店です。

Open for more than 50 years, the popular Takabashi Rāmen restaurant is one of Kyoto's oldest *rāmen* shops and is known for serving straight noodles with *shōyu*-based *tonkotsu* (pork stock) soup. Following renovations, the restaurant now features Ki-Yan's dynamic 'Sunflower' which enhances customers' *rāmen*-experience and adds some style to the eatery's motto of 'cheap, quick and delicious'. Though the restaurant has long been popular among *rāmen* fans in Kyoto, the vibrant atmosphere created by Ki-Yan's artwork has helped to increase Takabashi Rāmen's popularity among a wide range of customers. Experience dining at this modern *rāmen* restaurant with its sensational sunflower painting, innovative menu and polite, yet energetic staff!

1 豚骨スープの最初の清湯のみ使用した豚骨醤油味スープはあっさり風味。**2** 手作り餃子。**3** ガバチョ（豚バラ）。**4** 炒飯。
1 *Assari* (light) *rāmen* with *shōyu* and *tonkotsu* soup. **2** Homemade *gyōza* (dumplings) is a popular side dish. **3** *Gabacho*—a kind of *chāshū* (braised caramel pork belly). **4** *Chāhan* (fried rice)—a standard dish.

We feel sunshine all the time!

TAKABASHI RAMEN

map p166 -⑬
京都市中京区西ノ京桐尾町 1-6 BiVi 二条 1F
075-823-0114
11:00 ~ 24:00
無休
1 min walk from JR Nijō Sta
www.takabashi.com

クレヴィア京都四条後院通

4 KI-YAN STUZIO
祇園本店・祇園石段下店

がま口 / Gamaguchi Wallet

カップ＆ソーサー / Cup & Saucer 'Carp is Dragon in Heaven'

あづま袋「蛙と蓮」
Azuma Fukuro 'Frog and Lotus'

祇園石段下店 Gion Ishidanshita-ten

Ki-Yanの作品をアートグッズとして販売する「Ki-Yan Stuzio」は、バッグや洋服、インテリア、雑貨など様々な商品を取り揃えています。祇園本店には、獅子と牡丹のモザイクタイルやLED球で光る立体的な鯉などユニークな作品が並びます。両店の壁面にもKi-Yanワールドが満載。スタジオ（工房）としたのは「作品が生み出される場にしたかった」とKi-Yan。軽に集まり、グッズも並ぶスポットにしたかった」とKi-Yan。今後も面白いことが発信される場所になりそうです。

スマホケース / Smartphone Cover

ファブリック ショルダー
Fabric Shoulder Bag

5 KATSUKURA KYOTO STATION

かつくら 京都駅ビル The Cube 店

Lucky Bottlegourd

京都生まれのとんかつ「かつくら」は、ヘルシーな素材とカラッと軽やかな食感で大人気。各店で行列が絶えません。京都駅ビル店は2014年に口コミサイト・トリップアドバイザーで「外国人に人気の日本のレストラン ベスト30」にも選ばれ、海外からの利用者が急増。2015年には店内をリニューアルしました。商談の利用も多い外国人客のためにテーブル席を増やし、英語で接客するスタッフも揃えています。京野菜の鹿ケ谷かぼちゃと縁起のよいひょうたんは、Ki-Yanが京都の玄関口で魅せるもてなしの心です。

Originating in Kyoto, Katsukura has become a popular *tonkatsu* chain restaurant thanks to its healthy ingredients and the light and crispy texture of its fried food. With such popularity, it is no surprise to see queues outside of Katsukura outlets. In 2014 Katsukura was named one of TripAdvisor's top 30 restaurants in Kyoto, leading to a rapid increase in foreign customers. Renovating its Kyoto Station branch to serve larger numbers of foreign guests, Katsukura not only increased its number of seats, but also its English speaking staff. In addition, Ki-Yan's Kyoto vegetable motifs— *shishigatani* pumpkins and lucky bottle gourds—adorn the restaurant walls, welcoming travelers at 'Kyoto's gate'.

1 京都駅ビル The Cube 11Fのフロアで一段と目を引く鹿ケ谷かぼちゃ。**2** メインの料理を待つ間に自分好みのソース作り。**3** ボリュームたっぷり、名物かつくら膳。**4** 季節限定膳。山盛りのキャベツはおかわり自由。

1 Watch out for the blue *shishigatani* pumpkins dancing on the wall when walking through the 11th floor of Kyoto Station's Cube Food Court. **2** Make your own sauce while waiting for your main dish. **3** The famous Katsukura Zen set menu. **4** Seasonal Zen meal with miso soup, barley rice and free refills of shredded cabbage.

KATSUKURA KYOTO STATION

map p167 - ⑨

京都市下京区烏丸通
塩小路下ル 京都駅ビル
The Cube 11F

075-365-8666

11:00 ~ 22:00
テナント休館日

3 min walk from Kyoto Station
www.fukunaga-tf.com/katsukura

"I just want to create straightforward, simple, easy, free and rocking paintings."

WINE
RED

ストレートで、シンプルで、イージー、そして、フリーな、ロックな絵を描きたい。

CHAPTER 4

1. CHIRIRI 京都つゆしゃぶ CHIRIRI **68**
2. YAMASHITA 京・お漬物処 やました **70**
3. Wabiya Korekidō 侘家古暦堂 祇園花見小路本店 **72**
4. Restaurant VITRA レストラン ヴィトラ **74**
5. Katsukura Higashinotōin かつくら 四条東洞院店 **76**
6. NOUVELLE VAGUE KYOTO ヌーベルバーグ KYOTO **80**

Column 2 Rimpa 琳派 **82**

1 CHIRIRI

京都つゆしゃぶ CHIRIRI

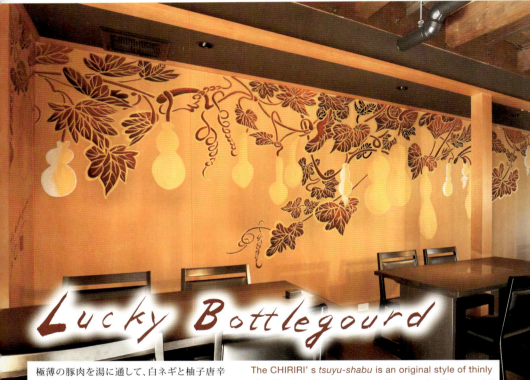

Lucky Bottlegourd

極薄の豚肉を湯に通して、白ネギと柚子唐辛子を入れた特製五段仕込みの和風のつゆだれでいただく「CHIRIRI」のつゆしゃぶ。もっともおいしい厚さだという0.8mmの極薄の肉と秘伝のつゆだれは、滋賀県にある本家の日本料理「ひょうたんや」で生まれた妙味です。しゃぶしゃぶを中心に、滋賀産の野菜や赤コンニャクなどが京都で味わえると大人気。ある夏の朝、Ki-Yanが京都府立植物園でスケッチしたというひょうたんは、この「CHIRIRI」での作品をきっかけにその後もよく描かれるモチーフになりました。

The CHIRIRI's *tsuyu-shabu* is an original style of thinly sliced pork boiled in water and flavoured with a special five-step *tsuyu* broth of white *negi* (spring onion) and *yuzukoshō* (a paste of chilli peppers and *yuzu* citrus peel). This exquisite flavour was first introduced at the Hyōtanya restaurant in Shiga, the prefecture where CHIRIRI originates. The most delicious flavours are achieved by using 0.8 mm thin slices of meat combined with the secret recipe for the *tsuyudare* sauce. Because of the delicious Shiga-grown vegetables and red *konnyaku* root, this original *shabu-shabu* has gained popularity in Kyoto as well. Ki-Yan's paintings of CHIRIRI's logo—the *hyōtan* (bottle gourd)—on the restaurant walls are based on several sketches drawn on a summer morning in the Kyoto Botanical Garden.

1 シックな空間に幸運のひょうたんが際立つ。スタッフの着物にもひょうたん柄。**2** 6つのつゆしゃぶコースが人気。**3** タイトルはKi-Yanらしくシンプルでストレート。

1 Look out for the bottle gourd motif on the waitresses' kimonos! Since painting at CHIRIRI, the bottle gourd has become one of Ki-Yan's favourite motifs. **2** Choose from the six most popular *tsuyu-shabu* courses. When the meat starts to make the sound 'chiri-chiri', it's ready to eat! **3** Another piece of Ki-Yan's work at the entrance of CHIRIRI – "The Black Panther of Hyōtanya".

I have Ki-Yan's 'Red Peony' on my phone!

CHIRIRI

map p166 - ⑪
京都市上京区大門町 265
075-222-5557
11:00 ~ 15:00
17:00 ~ 22:00 (Sun ~21:00)
reservations recommended
定休日 年末年始
3 min walk from Marutamachi Station, Karasuma subway line
http://chiriri.co.jp

2 YAMASHITA
京・お漬物処 やました

Flying Veggies

しば胡瓜　　南蛮胡瓜　　刻みすぐき

清水の産寧坂途中にある「京・お漬物処　やました」は、店主・山下弘行さんが亀岡市の畑で育てた野菜をメインに漬けた自家製の漬物店です。おいしさを追求した結果「野菜も自分で作りたい」と農業を始めて10年以上。スケッチを欠かさないKi-Yanは、京野菜を求め、山下さんの畑まで訪ねました。完成した壁画を見て山下さんが一番驚いたのは、野菜の葉。漬物にする部分ばかり気にかけてきたので、今まで見過ごしてきたその形の面白さを、改めてじっくり見ているとか。野菜作りからこだわった漬物は、熱意も染み込んだうまさです。

Offering homemade pickles made from fresh, locally grown vegetables, Tsukemono YAMASHITA is a Kyoto-based *tsukemono* (pickle) shop located on the Sannen-zaka Street near Kiyomizu-dera. The shop owner, Hiroyuki Yamashita, started his farm in Kameoka more than ten years ago with the purpose of making delicious pickles with his own *kyō-yasai* (Kyoto-grown vegetables). And you can surely taste the difference! Ki-Yan visited this farm for inspiration and, of course, to draw sketches for the mural. Even the owner, a devoted farmer and vegetable expert, was impressed by the resulting colourful, super-sized flying veggies on the walls of his shop.

My daikon radish is delicious!

1 日本人の食に欠かせない漬物。**2**「畑作業をしているときが一番カッコいい」とKi-Yan絶賛の山下さん。**3** 漬物はすべて試食可。歯ごたえがいい！**4** 賀茂茄子など京野菜が店内に飛び交う。

1 *Tsukemono* pickles—an essential accompaniment to Japanese dishes. **2** Mr Yamashita with his locally grown vegetables at his farm in Kameoka—the greatest inspiration for Ki-Yan's vibrant mural work. **3** Sample the different flavours and textures of YAMASHITA's *tsukemono*. **4** *Kamonasu* (a round-shaped Kyoto eggplant)—one of the Kyoto vegetables featured in the artwork.

YAMASHITA

map p166 -⑳

京都市東山区清水寺
門前産寧坂北入ル
清水3丁目316

075-561-8688

10:00 ~ 17:00
不定休

10 min walk from Kiyomizu-michi bus stop, bus 206 from Kyoto Station

www.kyo-yamashita.jp

3 WABIYA KOREKIDO
侘家古暦堂　祇園花見小路本店

オリジナルの侘家鶏を使った鶏料理を京都有数の花街・祇園にて提供する「侘家古暦堂 祇園花見小路本店」。有機野菜や無添加調味料など身体が喜ぶものだけを使ったおいしさです。2階の個室に描かれた黄金色の稲穂は「日本人の原点は米にある」というKi-Yanの想いと、祇園でお正月に芸妓・舞妓たちが髪に稲穂をつける慣習を重ね合わせて描かれました。豊かな実りに包まれた空間では、食事中の会話もいっそう楽しくはずみます。

Wabiya Korekidō Gion Hanami-kōji Honten (main branch) is a chicken speciality restaurant located in the heart of Gion's *geiko* (geisha) district. The restaurant cookes with the original *Wabiyadori* chicken brand along with organic vegetables and seasonings, using no additives. Ki-Yan chose the motif of the golden rice ear as a symbol of the origin of Japanese food culture. However, there is also a custom in the Gion district of decorating *geiko's* and *maiko's* hair with rice ears on New Year Day. The 'Gold Rice' painted on the wooden walls and sliding doors of the second floor, adds to the unique dining experience in this renovated *kyō-machiya* (Kyoto townhouse).

1 目の前で丁寧に焼かれる鶏肉。**2** 季節のおまかせコース。**3** 鳥をあしらった店のロゴマークは小粋。**4** 旬の野菜を炭火で焼いて食べる。

1 *Yakitori* (grilled chicken) is prepared right in front of guests at the counter on the first floor. **2** The seasonal *omakase* (chef's choice) course menu. **3** Coaster with the restaurant's original logo—Chinese characters of the restaurant's name designed in the form of stylized birds. **4** Fresh, seasonal charcoal grilled vegetables.

WABIYA KOREKIDO

map p165 -(28)

京都市東山区四条
花見小路下ル祇園町南側

075-532-3355

11:30 ~ 14:00
17:00 ~ 23:00
不定休

5 min walk from Gion Shijō Station, Keihan line or 7 min walk from Kawaramachi Station, Hankyū line

www.wabiya.com

5 KATSUKURA HIGASHINOTOIN
かつくら 四条東洞院店

ロースかつサンド
katsu sando for takeaway!

praise of barleycorn

2005年に描かれた、「かつくら 四条東洞院店」の作品「麦の賛歌」。同店で出される麦ご飯をモチーフに、豊穣の麦が店内で弾みます。とんかつや大海老かつ、湯葉巻かつなどメインが揚がるまで、すり鉢でゴマをすって待つスタイルはこのかつくらが最初です。店舗リニューアルの際に依頼されたこちらの壁画、実は短期間で仕上げる超過密なスケジュールで、かつくら本社デザイン室のスタッフも徹夜で参加。その一人は今、Team・Ki-Yanで大活躍している日本画家・武田修二郎氏です。

Ki-Yan painted 'The Praise of Barleycorn' at Katsukura's Higashinotōin branch in 2005. The barley motif, a symbol of fertility, comes from the signature style of Katsukura's rice—cooked with barley and served with crispy mains such as *tonkatsu* (breaded pork cutlets), *ōebikatsu* (prawn cutlets) and *yubakatsu* (tofu-skinned cutlets). Ki-Yan's mural painting was commissioned for the restaurant's reopening and completed in an extremely short time, just before the Gion Festival. Even members of Katsukura's head office's design department needed to work through the night to complete the project on time. One of them, the Nihonga artist Shūjirō Takeda, eventually became a member of Team Ki-Yan.

1 持ち帰りで人気の「かつくら かつサンド(ロースとヒレの2種類)」。**2**「とんかつ膳」。麦ご飯、みそ汁、キャベツはおかわり自由。**3** 調理場はガラス越しのオープンキッチン。**4** 季節メニューで多彩な湯葉コロッケや一品料理が登場。

1 Popular *katsu* sandwich comes in two varieties — pork loin and tenderloin. Also for takeaway. **2** *Tonkatsu zen* comes with unlimited refills of barley rice, miso soup and shredded cabbage. **3** Katsukura's open kitchen. **4** A Katsukura's seasonal dish: *yuba korokke* (tofu-skinned croquette).

1 とんかつソース、濃口ソース、ゆずドレッシングはお好みで。**2** 自分ですったゴマにソースを入れて、かつを待つ。**3** 店内の灯りのインテリアにもさりげなくKi-Yan。
1 Unbeatable dipping sauces: Katsukura's original sauce, spicy sauce and *yuzu* salad dressing. **2** At Katsukura's you can grind your own sesame seeds while waiting for the crispy mains. Mix the fragrant, freshly ground sesame with a sauce to make your own *tare* sauce. **3** Ki-Yan's motifs are also found on lampshades.

KATSUKURA HIGASHINOTOIN

map p164 - ⑨

京都市中京区東洞院通
四条上ル

075-221-4191

11:00 ~ 22:00
年中無休

5 min walk from Shijō Station,
Karasuma subway line

www.fukunaga-tf.com/
katsukura

6 NOUVELLE VAGUE KYOTO
ヌーベルバーグ KYOTO

オーナー・前場信之氏が学生時代に足しげく通い、スタッフになるほど惚れ込んだ料理店が無念の閉店。「なんとしてもこの味を伝えたい」とオープンしたのが、この「ヌーベルバーグKYOTO」です。受け継いだ料理の中でも「タルトタタン」はとくに思い入れのあるメニューだそう。当時のレシピ通り、15cmホールに4～5個のリンゴを使い10時間かけて作ります。Ki-Yanは、実際に料理に使われている品種"フジ"を選んでリンゴの絵を描くというこだわりよう。細やかな丁寧さが光ります。

NOUVELLE VAGUE is a Kyoto café restaurant, which celebrates its signature dish of Tarte Tatin. Spending his university days dining and eventually working at a restaurant in Kyoto, the owner of NOUVELLE VAGUE, Mr Nobuyuki Maeba, decided to open his own culinary business upon the closing of the restaurant. Inspired by his previous workplace, the Tarte Tatin is NOUVELLE VAGUE's most impressive dish. Following the original recipe, it takes Mr Maeba 10 hours to transform 4-5 apples into one 15 cm round tart. Fuji apples are used in both the tarts and the artwork—Ki-Yan travelled all the way to Nagano Prefecture to make the sketches for this piece. You can spot Ki-Yan's apples painted on the big industrial fridge in the La Village branch of NOUVELLE VAGUE.

1 カフェレストランとテイクアウトの「ヌーベルバーグ KYOTO」(京都市役所隣り)。**2** タルトタタンはテイクアウトも可。**3** テイクアウト専門「ヌーベルバーグ KYOTO ラ・ヴィラージュ」でタルトタタンを作るオーナー。**4**「ヌーベルバーグ KYOTO」は白を基調にした落ち着いた店内。**5** 温めたタルトタタンにはヨーグルトを添えて。

1 NOUVELLE VAGUE KYOTO, Teramachi street branch. **2** Tarte Tatin for takeaway. **3** Mr Maeba making the Tarte Tatin in the La Village branch of NOUVELLE VAGUE in Sagano, specialized in takeaway. **4** Enjoy the Tarte Tatin in NOUVELLE VAGUE's café branch on Teramachi Street. **5** Hot Tarte Tatin with yogurt topping.

Tarte Tatin, yummm...!

NOUVELLE VAGUE KYOTO

map p164 - ①

京都市中京区寺町御池
上ル上本能寺町 473
浅井ビル 1F

075-741-8734

11:00 ~ 22:30
closed Tuesday

3 min walk from Shiyakusho-mae Station, Tōzai subway line

www.nouvelle-kyoto.com

NOUVELLE VAGUE KYOTO LA VILLAGE

map p166 - ㉗

京都市右京区嵯峨
折戸町 24-29

075-864-8572

10:00 ~ 19:30
closed Tuesday

2 min walk from Rokuōin Station, Keifuku (Randen) line or 5 min walk from Saga-Arashiyama Station, JR line

www.nouvelle-kyoto.com

COLUMN 2

RIMPA
琳派

　2015年は本阿弥光悦が鷹峯に光悦村を拓いて400年。琳派400年記念イベントに、琳派の遺伝子を継ぐ絵師として私も参加することになった。染織などで様式化した"琳派もどき"を琳派は避けてきたが、俵屋宗達だけは別格だ。

　美術館展示を最終目的にする現代の美術界に疑問を持っていた。私はポップアート、街を行く人たちからカッコいいと言われたい。だから「Ki-Yan Stuzio」を展開した。

　世界に類例をみない琳派の元祖でもある俵屋宗達も、扇子や屏風などを描く町絵師だったと聞く。為政者にかかえられたのではなく、町衆に育まれた。京の町衆はただの金持ちは認めない。アートを理解し、新しき美意識をもつ商人だけが大旦那として尊敬された。こんな風潮が宗達、そして琳派を生むのである。どこかヴェニスの商人たちと似ている。

2015 commemorates 400 years since Hon'ami Kōetsu founded the Rimpa artistic community in Takagamine, Kyoto. As a painter who inherited the Rimpa spirit, I am participating in some of the events celebrating the school's 400th anniversary. I do not like to be categorized as a 'Rimpa artist' as the style is also used for 'fake Rimpa', especially in the textile arts. However, I have great respect for Tawaraya Sōtatsu.

I have had doubts about the contemporary art world, whose ultimate aim is to exhibit art in art museums. Like in the case of pop art, I would like people on the street to call my art 'cool'. That is why I opened the Ki-Yan Stuzio.

Tawaraya Sōtatsu, the founder of the unique Rimpa art movement, also painted on folding screens or fans for the common people. He was not supported by the rulers, but by the wealthy merchants of Kyoto. However, being rich was not enough to be an art sponsor: only merchants who had aesthetic sense and an understanding for art were respected as partons and called *ōdanna*. Sōtatsu and Rimpa were born in this atmosphere, reminiscent of the art patronage in Renaissance Venice.

乾きが速い。色が鮮明で乾くと取れない。水性で扱い易い。アクリル絵の具は、エレキギターに似ている。

WHITE
SILVER

"Acrylic paint is like an electric guitar. It dries quickly, once dry is hard to remove, and is water-based, so easy to use. The variety of vivid colours is virtually endless."

CHAPTER 5

1. Piito 四十（ピート） **86**
2. Chōrakukan 長楽館 コーラル **88**
3. TOKU 和牛焼肉 徳 **92**
4. Kyoto Hatoya 京湯元 ハトヤ瑞鳳閣 **94**
5. ADACHI 京の惣菜 あだち **98**
6. Nakagyō Police Station 京都府警 中京警察署 **102**
7. Yume Kōbō Kyō 夢工房 京 三年坂店 **104**
8. Toh-Lee からすま京都ホテル 中国料理 桃李 **106**
9. Taisushi 江戸前にぎり 鯛寿司 **110**
10. Kyoto Medical Center 京都医療センター **112**

1 PIITO
匹十（ピート）

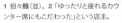

1 担々麺（並）。**2**「ゆったりと座れるカウンター席にもこだわった」という店主。
1 Piito's *tantan* noodle soup. **2** Enjoy comfortable counter seating while chatting to the owner of this cosy noodle shop.

京都三条商店街の中に象がいる!?　買い物客らの視線を集めているのは、担々麺「匹十」の店頭で飛んでいる白い象。野菜をベースにしたまろやかな風味は辛味が苦手な方にもおすすめです。

ユニークな店名は海外ドラマの主人公の名前"ピート"の当て字なんだそう。店名を逆にした10匹の象は、方位にこだわるKi-Yanらしく運気上昇の乾（西北）に向けて描かれました。店内でも見られるようにとガラスの両面にペインティングされた象たちは、店主の元気のもとになっています。

Have you seen Ki-Yan's 'Flying Elephants' on Kyoto's famous Sanjō Shōtengai shopping street? If so, there is no surprise that the *tantan* noodle shop intrigues every passer-by, offering not-too-spicy *tantan* noodles topped with plenty of fresh vegetables. The shop's unique name 'Piito' originates from Pete Lattimer, the hero of the owner's favourite U.S. TV drama 'Warehouse 13'. The ten elephants are the result of a play on words of the two Chinese characters used for the shop's name which can be read as 'ten animals' when inverted. Additionally, the elephants are facing the direction of northwest as a symbol of luck. As Ki-Yan painted the elephant motifs on both sides of the large shop window, you can enjoy the artwork from inside as well!

PIITO

map p166 - ⑭

京都市中京区西ノ京
南聖町 4-13

075-842-1129

11:30 ~ 15:00
closed Monday

5 min walk from Nijō Station,
JR line or Tōzai subway line

2 CHORAKUKAN
長楽館 コーラル

Love Doves

レストランウェディングでは憧れの的、円山公園そばの「長楽館コーラル」には、慶びの場にふさわしく平和と愛の鳩が羽ばたいています。その数はなんと650羽。Team・Ki-Yanがまだ結成していない頃、わずかな制作期間にKi-Yanの友人たちが協力して完成させた大作の一つです。形が微妙な鳩もご愛嬌。みんなの愛で包まれた空間が多くの新しい門出を祝福します。長楽館100周年の際には旧館と新館をつなぐ回廊にファンタスティックな孔雀も登場。訪れる人を幸せへと導いています。

Located near Kyoto's Maruyama Park, Chōrakukan's Italian restaurant Coral, is a popular and trendy venue for 'restaurant weddings'. With 650 'Love Doves' flying across the walls and ceiling, the restaurant provides a stylish and romantic setting for weddings. The impressive large-scale mural painting was completed in a very short time with the help of Ki-Yan's friends—before the founding of Team Ki-Yan. So while some of the doves are not perfect, they are still charming! To commemorate Chōrakukan's 100th anniversary, in 2008 Ki-Yan painted gorgeous peacocks in the passage between the old and new buildings to bring fortune to newlywed couples.

1 メニューにもKi-Yanの孔雀が羽を広げる。2 シェフのおすすめランチ・前菜。3 メインの魚料理。旬の素材が楽しめる。

1 The restaurant's menu decorated with Ki-Yan's peacock. **2** A chef recommended lunch menu entrée. **3** Fish served with fresh seasonal ingredients.

Have you ever tried Kyoto style Italian cuisine?

Darling Peacock

The story began with Peacock brand cigarettes!

1 明治時代のたばこ「ピーコック」にちなんで描かれた孔雀。2 長楽館のコースター。同館は煙草王・村井吉兵衛が迎賓館として建築した。3 笑顔の素敵な土手千果さん。お母様は長楽館オーナーの土手素子さん。

1 The motif of the peacock comes from the tobacco brand Peacock—owned by Kichibei Murai, the former owner of Chōrakukan's guesthouse. **2** Coasters designed after vintage tobacco packages—for sale as souvenirs. **3** The charming Chika Dote—a Chōrakukan employee and the daughter of the current owner of Chōrakukan, Motoko Dote.

CHŌRAKUKAN

map p165 - ㉕
京都市東山区八坂鳥居前
東入ル円山町 604

075-561-0001

11:30 ~ 14:00
17:30 ~ 20:00
不定休

5 min walk from Gion bus stop, bus 206 from Kyoto Station or 10 min walk from Gion Shijō Station, Keihan line

www.chourakukan.co.jp

3 TOKU

和牛焼肉 徳

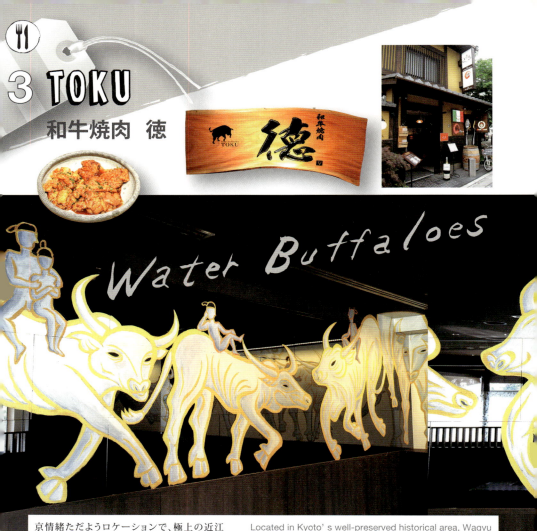

京情緒ただようロケーションで、極上の近江牛をリーズナブルに味わえる「和牛焼肉 徳」では、Ki-Yan作品初のモチーフ・水牛を見ることができます。選りすぐりのA4・A5ランクのお肉は、赤身とサシ（脂身）のバランスが絶妙。掘りごたつの和モダンな空間には、アジアの生活風景をイメージして描いたという水牛と戯れる人々の絵が食の宴を盛り上げています。
やわらかくて旨みたっぷりのお肉で満腹になった帰りには、天空へとかけ昇る金の鯉がお見送り。「口福」のもてなしと粋な計らいが魅力のお店です。

Located in Kyoto's well-preserved historical area, Wagyu Yakiniku TOKU serves reasonably priced, carefully selected and the highest quality A4 and A5 grade *Ōmi gyū* (purebred brand wagyu beef from Shiga prefecture). Ki-Yan's featured artwork depicts a South Asian landscape with a new motif of water buffaloes painted on the mirrored partition walls of the main modern Japanese dining space with *horigotatsu*-style sunken seating. Though you are bound to be satisfied with the authentic, tender, melt in your mouth wagyu bites and the restaurant's superior *omotenashi* (hospitality), don't forget to check out another Ki-Yan mural 'Carp is Dragon in Heaven'. It is one of artist's favourite motifs and is best seen on your way down the stairs.

1 帰り際にチェック！ Ki-Yan作の昇る鯉。2 上質の近江牛を堪能。3 掘りごたつのテーブル席は足元もゆったり。4 本日の逸品は来てのお楽しみ！ 5 徳こだわりのタレにつけられた、和牛のタレ3種盛り。

1 The golden rising carp painting—check it out on your way down the stairs! **2** Enjoy top quality *Ōmi gyū*. **3** TOKU's popular *horigotatsu*-style seating. **4** Daily special served in a beautiful lacquered *bento* box. **5** Three kinds of wagyu meat marinated in TOKU's homemade *tare* sauce.

TOKU

map p165 - ⑧

京都市東山区大和
大路通三条下ル
3丁目弁財天町26

075-533-2929

17:00 ~ 24:00
closed Monday

5 min walk from Gion-Shijō Station, Keihan line or 7 min walk from Kawaramachi Station, Hankyū line

www.nawate-kyoto.jp/toku

4 KYOTO HATOYA
Kyoto Hot Spring Hatoya Zuihōkaku Hotel
京湯元　ハトヤ瑞鳳閣

2014年に全館建替えでリニューアルした「京湯元　ハトヤ瑞鳳閣」。最上階にある天然温泉の大浴場には、湯けむりの中でも際立つ縁起物のひょうたんと南天、そして雲錦（桜と紅葉）が広がります。Team・Ki-Yanが滋賀県信楽へ出向き、60cm四方の陶板に特殊な塗料で絵つけしたという珍しい作品で、地下910mから汲み上げる自家源泉の温泉でくつろぐ人たちの心をほぐします。屋上に移された工事中の囲い壁に羽ばたく鳩1220羽は必見。そのまま空高く舞い上がりそうなパワーを放っています。

The newly reconstructed Hatoya Hot Spring Zuihōkaku Hotel reopened in 2014 and features Ki-Yan's work in the large bath of the *onsen* (hot springs) on the top floor. Filled with water collected from 910 meters below ground, the *onsen* offers you an opportunity to relax while gazing upon Ki-Yan's lucky motifs of bottle gourds, *nanten* (nandin) and *unkin* (*sakura* cherry blossoms and Japanese maple leaves). To create this unusual piece of art, Team Ki-Yan travelled to Shigaraki in Shiga prefecture and used a special technique to paint these lucky motifs on 60cm on 4 sides ceramic plates. While at Hatoya you can find another piece of Ki-Yan's work: a wall painted with 1220 doves. Initially a temporary wall put up around construction work, the piece was eventually moved to Hatoya's roof garden for permanent display.

1 京都の景色をパクッ!「ハトヤ瑞鳳閣オリジナル落雁」。**2** オリジナルキャラクター・はとピヨンは総支配人の岩井依子さんデザイン。コースターにも登場。**3** はとピヨンのストラップ。**4** 日帰りの温泉利用にも便利なエコバッグ。**5** ハトヤ瑞鳳閣をイメージした鳩の屏風。
1 Hatoya's original *rakugan* (a hard sweet made of soybean and rice flour mixed with sugar) decorated with Kyoto motifs. **2, 3, 4** A coaster, strap and reusable shopping bag featuring Hatoya's original character Hatopyon, designed by general manager Yoriko Iwai. **5** *Byobu* folding screen decorated with Ki-Yan's doves.

恐れ入ります切手をお貼り下さい

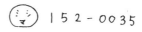 152-0035

東京都目黒区自由が丘
2-6-13
株式会社 ミシマ社
編集部 行

フリガナ		
お名前	男性 女性	歳

〒

ご住所

☎ (　　　)

お仕事・学校名

メルマガ登録ご希望の方は是非お書き下さい。

E-mail

※携帯のアドレスは登録できません。ご了承下さいませ。

★ ご記入いただいた個人情報は、今後の出版企画の参考として以外は利用致しません。

ご購入、誠にありがとうございます。
ご感想、ご意見を お聞かせ下さい。

① この本の書名

② この本をお求めになった書店

③ この本をお知りになったきっかけ

④ ご感想をどうぞ

＊お客様のお声は、新聞、雑誌広告、HPで匿名にて掲載
させていただくことがございます。ご了承ください。

⑤ ミシマ社への一言

1 屋上で羽ばたく1220羽の鳩。1220は、ハトヤ瑞鳳閣の社長とKi-Yanが出会った「平安建都1200」のイベントから20年後のリニューアルにちなんだ数字。2 夏は京都タワーをのぞみながら、ビアガーデンで乾杯!(期間限定・予約制) 3 Ki-Yanの鳩がデザインされた宿泊客用の浴衣も。

1 Hatoya's roof garden. The 1220 doves represent the 1220th anniversary of the founding of Kyoto, celebrated in 2014—the year of the hotel's reopening. 2 Enjoy a stunning view of the Kyoto Tower while having a rooftop drink during Kyoto's hot summer season (reservations required). 3 Ki-Yan's doves are also found on guests' *yukata*.

KYOTO HATOYA

map p167 - ⑦

京都市下京区西洞院通
塩小路下ル南不動堂町
802

075-361-1231
(hotel reservation)

check-in   from 14:00
check-out   until 10:00

5 min walk from Kyoto Station

www.kyoto-hatoya.jp

5 ADACHI
京の惣菜 あだち

京都の家庭の味・おばんざいを中心に、和洋中のメニューを取り入れた手作りの味が並ぶ「あだち」。旬の素材をいかしたお惣菜は量り売りで、ランチ、お酒も楽しめる夜ご飯など自由なスタイルで味わうことができます。日々の手軽なおかずは、創業当時の1951年から60年以上経った今も、常連さんから観光客まで訪れる親しみのある味です。店頭のガラスに躍る京野菜と魚は、店内の壁画を描き終えたKi-Yanが急遽追加したもの。道行く人から視線を集めています。

This family-owned restaurant offers mainly *obanzai* (traditional Kyoto cuisine) style Japanese, Chinese and Western homemade dishes made with fresh seasonal ingredients and sold by weight. Choose freely from the various lunch and dinner menu items, or find those items that best complement your choice of sake. Founded in 1951, Adachi has maintained its popularity among locals as well as domestic and foreign tourists. The restaurant features an iconic window of Ki-Yan's flying *kyō yasai* (Kyoto vegetables) and seafood—images that suddenly came to the artist just after finishing the impressive murals inside the restaurant.

1 日替わりランチはメイン1品に惣菜が3品選べて味噌汁付き。100円プラスで女将こだわりのコーヒーor紅茶が付く。**2** 惣菜はどれも手頃な価格。好きな分量だけ買える。**3** しっかりとした風味が持ち味。京都の家庭料理は実はそれほど薄味ではない。**4** 三代目と四代目で仲良く店を切り盛り。

1 Lunch sets include your choice of three dishes and one daily special served with miso soup and rice. Add tea or coffee to your order for an extra 100 yen. **2** A wide selection of reasonably priced dishes are displayed in the cabinet and are sold by weight. **3** Adachi's dishes are known for their rich flavours. **4** Two generations of the Adachi family.

1 Ki-Yanの京野菜が弾む。2 アンティークな家具やディスプレイは四代目若主人のこだわり。3 惣菜と同じく手作り感あふれる「今日のメニュー」をチェックして中へ。4 この界隈は平安京の内裏があったところ。

1 Dancing Kyoto vegetables—Chinese cabbage, *manganji* pepper and *ebiimo* (a kind of taro) on the restaurant's walls. 2 The forth generation owners' antique furniture and other favourite interior items. 3 *Obanzai*—home-style dishes made fresh daily and posted on the changing menu board. 4 Ki-Yan's paintings invite you to visit a historical area—ADACHI's neighbourhood was once the site of the Imperial Palace.

ADACHI

map p166 -⑩

京都市上京区千本
丸太町東入ル
075-841-4156
12:00 ~ 14:30 lunch
18:30 ~ 22:00 dinner
11:00 ~ 18:30 takeaway
closed Sunday
10 min walk from JR Nijō Station or 2 min walk from Senbonmarutamachi bus stop, bus 206 from Kyoto Station
www.kyoto-adachi.jp

map p166 - ⑮

White Tigers 103

7 YUME KOBO KYO
夢工房 京 三年坂店

甘い香りまで漂ってきそうな大輪のカサブランカが見つめるのは、あこがれの舞妓、芸妓、花魁などに変身して華やぐ女性たち。本格的なメイク、衣装、撮影が産寧坂という京情緒あふれる観光スポットで体験できると大人気のお店です。最近は、日本の伝統文化をダイレクトに体感できると外国人の利用者も増加。華麗に咲き誇るKi-Yan作のカサブランカの前は、撮影のベストスポット。だれもが幸せ気分で最高の笑顔を見せる空間になっています。

Upon entering the studio Yume Kōbō Kyō, every woman willing to transform herself into an adorable *maiko*, *geiko* (the Kyoto word for geisha) or *oiran* is welcomed with Ki-Yan's giant Casablanca lilies—so life-like that you can almost smell their fragrance! This *maiko* makeover studio is not only popular because of its professional make-up, dress-up and photo shooting services, but because of its location in the Sannen-zaka area, one of Kyoto's most popular sightseeing districts. Both Japanese and foreigners can enjoy experiencing traditional Japanese culture first-hand by strolling through the streets of Kyoto dressed in kimono. You can also request your photo be taken with your own camera, and the best spot for your glamour shot is the red sofa in front of Ki-Yan's 'Darling Casablancas'!

1 変身写真でキーホルダーも作れる。 2 舞妓変身が一番人気。 3 カサブランカはお店のシンボルに。

1 Order an original keychain with your *maiko henshin* (*maiko* makeover) shot. **2** The *maiko henshin* is the studio's most popular plan. **3** Ki-Yan's Casablanca lily motif also appears on the studio's flyer.

Experience being Maiko or Geisha! Foreigners welcome!

YUKE KOBO KYO

map p166 -⑲

京都市東山区清水
3丁目 327-6

075-531-1140

10:00 ~ 19:00
reservations until 17:00

無休

10 min walk from Kiyomizu-michi bus stop, bus 206 from Kyoto Station

www.maiko-kyo.jp

8 TOH-LEE
からすま京都ホテル 中国料理 桃李

広東料理をベースにした京都らしい上品な中国料理で人気の、からすま京都ホテル「中国料理 桃李」。ランチ、ディナーともに、長年幅広い層から支持されるレストランです。烏丸通りに面した明るい客席には、訪れる人を静かに迎える気持ちを込めてあえて色目を抑えたという「阿吽のトラ」。アジアの料理には獅子（ライオン）よりもトラがいいというKi-Yan流の解釈です。また個室では本物の竹の合間から、威嚇しつつも茶目っ気のある表情をのぞかせるシルバーのトラたちが、円卓を囲む人々を和ませています。

Located in the Kyoto Karasuma Hotel, the Chinese restaurant Toh-Lee serves elegant Kyoto style dishes based on Cantonese cuisine. Both lunch and dinner have maintained a long-standing popularity with a wide range of customers. Restaurant guests are welcomed by Ki-Yan's set of two A-Un Tigers hanging near the windows facing Karasuma Street. These tigers are the artist's playful interpretation of *komainu* (guardian lion-dogs)—the paired animal statues usually found at the entrance of Japanese shrines and temples. However, Toh-Lee's private room holds the artist's main work: the cute but dangerous-looking silver tigers—painted on an ice-green wall behind real bamboo—who will be watching you as you dine at the round table.

1 ミラーアクリルに白と銀で描かれた「阿吽のトラ」。 2 ランチで人気の「飲茶セット」。3 凄味を利かせつつも心はwelcomeなトラ。

1 'Aun-A Tiger' with an open mouth. Both tigers are painted on acrylic mirrors. 2 A popular yum cha set menu for lunch. 3 'Aun-Un Tiger' with a closed mouth.

1 Ki-Yanが「壁が自分では使わない色で面白いから（依頼に）乗った」というアイスグリーンの個室。シャンデリアにもよく合うからトラにはシルバーが使われた。**2** 3種盛りの飲茶も熱々で。**3** マンゴープリンとゴマ団子。**4** デザートは杏仁豆腐。大満足！

1 'As I don't usually use green as a background for my paintings, I felt challenged to take on this job,' explains Ki-Yan. The artist used silver for the tigers to match with the private room's chandeliers. **2** A set of three different yum cha dumplings. **3** Fried sweet sesame dumpling and mango pudding. **4** Another dessert? How about almond jelly with fruit!

1

3

4

TOH-LEE

map p164 -26

京都市下京区烏丸通
四条下ル

075-371-0141

11:00 ~ 14:30
11:00 ~ 15:00 (Sat & Sun)
17:30 ~ 21:00

0 min walk from Shijō Station,
Karasuma subway line, exit 6

http://karasuma.
kyotohotel.co.jp

9 TAISUSHI
江戸前にぎり 鯛寿司

気軽にのれんをくぐれる、「江戸前にぎり 鯛寿司」。大将と女将の2人が、何十年と通う常連客から一見客まで丁寧に接客をしてくれます。寿司はおまかせが基本、外せないのは名物ねぎま汁と炙り穴子です。Ki-Yanも長年通っていたこの店。2014年に50周年を迎え、その記念にと依頼されたのが棚のガラス戸です。サンドブラストによる寿司ネタで、「絵を描く素材や形、スタイルに興味があるからガラスでもやってみたかった」という作品は、小ぶりながらも存在感があります。

Based on a special request made by Taisushi's owner, the restaurant has decided not to provide an introduction in English, as it is not able to accommodate non-Japanese speaking customers.

'As we are not able to provide any service or explanation in English, we ask those requiring English assistance to choose a different sushi bar. Thank you for your understanding.'

Taisushi's Owner

1 ふわふわの食感がたまらない炙り穴子。2 鯛寿司名物のねぎま汁。少し時間がかかるので早目に注文を。3 お造りはその日のおすすめをおまかせで。4 額の作品は珍しい、Ki-Yanの鯛と蛸。5 ガラス戸の作品の下絵がこちら。定番の寿司ネタがモチーフに。

TAISUSHI

map p165 - (14)

京都市中京区四条
河原町上ル一筋目
東入ル

075-221-6598

17:00 ~ 22:00
closed Thursday

3 min walk from Kawara-machi Station, Hankyū line

"I would rather be seen as 'cool' by the people on the street than be appreciated by art critics or famous painters."

MULTI
COLOUR

高名な評論家や
巨匠に評価されるよりも、
街行く人に、カッコいい
と言われたい。

CHAPTER 6

1. Doyanen どやねん **116**
2. Kyoto Travelers Inn 京都トラベラーズ・イン **118**
3. WAZAGU 京都国際工芸センター **120**
4. eX cafe 京都嵐山本店 **122**
5. Takashimaya 京都タカシマヤ **126**
6. Morikō ぎをん森幸 **128**
7. KOTOWA 京都八坂 **132**
8. GION WABIZA 祇園倭美坐 **134**
9. BAR HANARE 駒屋 花れ家 **136**
10. TANA-X 株式会社タナックス **138**
11. Jūrokudai Gondayu 十六代権太夫 **140**
12. The Aglio Garden アーリオガーデン **144**
13. Daichakai 祇園大茶會 **146**

Column 3 Japanese Feng Shui 方位学 **148**

1 DOYANEN
どやねん

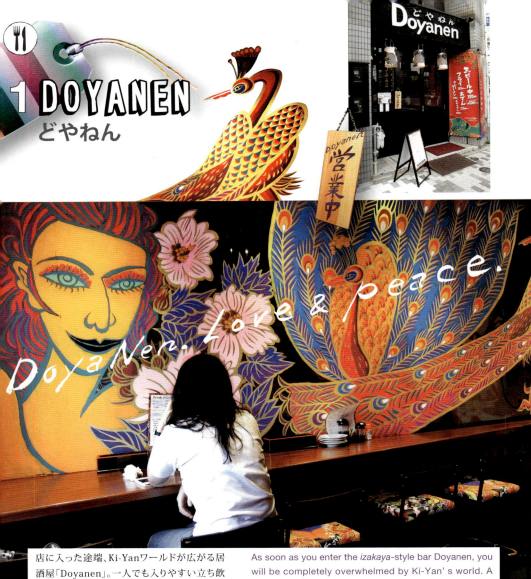

店に入った途端、Ki-Yanワールドが広がる居酒屋「Doyanen」。一人でも入りやすい立ち飲み感覚のリーズナブルさが、学生や仕事帰りのサラリーマン、女性客、地元のちょい飲み派などにも好評です。「お客さんをすっぽり絵で包み込むぐらいの迫力で描きたかった」というKi-Yan。これまでの作品を大集合させた賑やかな壁面ですが、見逃せないのは女性のモチーフで、今のところはこの店のみ。クールビューティーな瞳で酔客を見つめる視線に、思わずもう一杯か、もうやめとこか……はあなた次第。

As soon as you enter the *izakaya*-style bar Doyanen, you will be completely overwhelmed by Ki-Yan's world. A quick drink at this reasonably priced street-vendor-stall atmosphere eatery is popular among students, women, Japanese salarymen and local social drinkers. 'My intention was to wrap the customers in my paintings', says Ki-Yan. The artist's work here features almost all of his painting motifs of plants and animals, but the women's faces are a novelty and—at the moment—can only be encountered at Doyanen. Experience Ki-Yan's unique imagery and indulge in one more drink while being watched by the 'cool beauties' on the wall.

1 微笑みに乾杯！現在はテーブル席として賑わっている。**2** 佐々木酒造とコラボしたフルーティーで飲みやすい「平安四神」。**3** 京の鰻の寝床を思わせる奥に細長い店内。**4**「アンチかわいい〜！」を主張する成熟した女性。**5** トイレもKi-Yanによる「Doyanen」仕様。**6** おでんと並ぶ人気の串カツはお持ち帰りもできる。

1 This former counter now provides table seating beside the huge mural just left of the entrance. **2** 'Four Gods of the Heian Period' label design by Ki-Yan in collaboration with the sake brewery Shuzō Sasaki. **3** The long, narrow interior of DOYANEN resembles 'eel beds' found in traditional Kyoto townhouses. **4** The mature blue-faced woman as an expression of Ki-Yan's 'anti-*kawaii*' philosophy. **5** Watch out for KI-Yan's motifs in the restroom as well! **6** *Oden* (hotpot dish) and *kushikatsu* (skewered and grilled meat)— also available for takeaway.

6 oden (hotpot dish)

6 kushikatsu skewers

DOYANEN

map p166 - (24)

京都市左京区下鴨本
通北小路北西角 11-8

075-746-6879

**17:00 ~ 24:00
closed Thursday**

1min walk from Rakuhoku
kōkō-mae bus stop,
bus 206 from Kyoto Station

https://ja-jp.facebook.com/doyanenken

2 KYOTO TRAVELERS INN
京都トラベラーズ・イン

琵琶湖疏水に面し、美術館や図書館などが集まる京都の文化ゾーンで、リーズナブルに旅をサポート。2014年に車椅子対応など館内をリニューアルし、より良い滞在を提供しています。だれもが思わず見上げるフロントとカフェのフロアもその一つ。すぐそばにある平安神宮の神苑(日本庭園)から飛来してきたイメージで、牡丹、芙蓉、糸菊、椿が空間いっぱいに描かれています。見逃せないのはフロント前のトイレ。洗面台前の鏡に映る、自分の姿の後ろには……Ki-Yanの遊び心に思わず感動!

Located in Kyoto's picturesque Okazaki district—renowned for the Heian-jingū Shrine, museums, libraries and other cultural institutions—and facing the historical Lake Biwa Canal, Travelers Inn offers reasonably priced accommodation. The hotel reopened in 2014 following renovation, offering wheelchair access and attracting visitors with Ki-Yan's impressive murals on the walls and ceiling of the reception and Cafe Green Box. The flowers used in this work were inspired by the garden of the neighbouring Heian-jingū, and symbolize the four seasons: peony for spring, cotton rose for summer, itogiku chrysanthemum for autumn, and camellia for winter.

1 茶葉は「Ashiya Proud」。10色揃ったティーポットもかわいい。2 カフェメニューには豚肉を含まないスープなども用意。3 朝に咲いて夕方にしぼむ"1日花"の芙蓉。Ki-Yanの芙蓉はずっと咲いて楽しめる。

1 Choose from a selection of Ashiya Proud Japanese teas. Enjoy the teapots, available in ten colours. **2** Cafe Green Box offers soups made from locally produced vegetables, mainly organic. Halal and vegan menu items available. **3** Ki-Yan's cotton rose – a summer flower, known for blooming for only one day. In spring, experience real *sakura* cherry blossoms just in front of Travelers Inn, one of the most popular *sakura*-viewing spots in Kyoto!

KYOTO TRAVELERS INN

map p167 -②

京都市左京区岡崎
円勝寺町 91

075-771-0225

check-in　from 15:00
check-out　until 10:00

7 min walk from Higashiyama Station or Keage Station, Tōzai subway line

www.k-travelersinn.com

4 EX CAFE
eX cafe 京都嵐山本店

観光地・嵐山の喧騒を忘れそうなゆったりした空間が広がるのは、昭和初期の旧邸宅を改装した「eX cafe 京都嵐山本店」。重厚な門の奥には黒壁に黒い牡丹の粋な絵が出迎えます。制作時にはワインレッドだった葉っぱが経年変化で鮮やかな青色になったのはKi-Yanもびっくり。約400㎡の日本庭園をソファ席やテーブル席、座敷などいろんなスタイルで眺められます。人気の「京黒ロールくろまる」や「天龍寺パフェ」を楽しみに、芸能人や有名人も頻繁に訪れるそう。赤と白の獅子の座敷はぜひ家族連れで!

Converted from an early Showa period home, this large coffee house offers a quiet space to relax within Kyoto's bustling tourist hub of Arashiyama. Upon entering the Japanese style gates, guests will encounter Ki-Yan's elegant 'Black Peony' painted on the building's black façade. The artist himself was surprised to find that the original wine red colour of the peony's leaves transformed to vivid blue only a few years after the work's completion. Offering both Western and tatami style rooms as well as Japanese garden views, the eX cafe Arashiyama is favoured not only by tourists, but celebrities as well. Sit crossed-legged on a tatami mat while enjoying your dessert and viewing Ki-Yan's red and white lions in the cafe's Japanese style room.

1 左ページが現在の青色の葉。右ページは制作当初のワインレッドの葉。 **2** お土産用の「京黒ロールくろまる」はここでしか買えない。 **3** 竹炭入りの真黒なスポンジにたっぷりの白いクリーム。

1 Wine red leaves of the black peony just after finishing the mural in 2010. Left page: Current vivid blue colour of the leaves. **2** The famous *Kyō-kuro-rōru-kuromaru* souvenir cake, sold only here. **3** *Kyō-kuro-rōru-kuromaru* – eX cafe's original soft sponge roll cake, baked with bamboo charcoal and filled with white cream.

1 赤獅子に見つめられてドキドキしそうな席。2 京黒ロールくろまるドリンクセット。3 天龍寺パフェセット。4 赤獅子と黒い牡丹の掛軸。5 父親に甘える子どもが愛らしい白獅子の座敷。

1 Seating just beside the red lion's *fusuma* sliding door paintings. 2 Set dessert menu of *Kyō-kuro-rōru-kuromaru* cake with choice of drink. 3 *Tenryūji* parfait. 4 Ki-Yan's 'Red Lion and Black Peony' *kakejiku* hanging scroll decorates the tatami room. 5 White baby lions playing on their father's back on the *fusuma* of the tatami room.

EX CAFE

map p166 - 26

京都市右京区嵯峨天龍寺造路町 35-3

075-882-6366

10:00 ~ 18:00
不定休

1 min walk from Arashiyama Station, Keifuku (Randen) line

www.inden-style.jp

6 MORIKO
ぎをん森幸

Cotton Roses & Peacock

香辛料に頼らない、あっさりとした風味の京風中華料理が味わえる「ぎをん森幸」。1955年の開店当時から先代が得意とした春巻、大海老の天ぷら、酢豚、ふかひれスープなど、どれを食べてもウマイッ。現店主・森田恭規さんが始めた、辛みがクセになる麻婆豆腐も常連客が外さない人気メニューです。「ここはオレンジ色を基調にしよう」。それだけを決めてあとは感じたままを描いたというKi-Yan。毎日見ている森田さんは、絵が描かれて7年経った今も、孔雀と芙蓉から元気をもらっている気がするそうです。

Gion Morikō serves Kyoto style Chinese cuisine with a less spicy and *assari* (light) taste. Since opening in 1955, this restaurant has been famous for its signature dishes including fried spring rolls, lobster tempura, *subuta* (sweet and sour pork) and shark soup. The *mābōdōfu* (or mapo tofu) offered by the current owner-chef Yasunori Morita has become very popular among regulars and new customers alike. Ki-Yan spontaneously used orange for this peacock motif as he felt it would match well with the food and atmosphere of this vibrant Chinese restaurant. The gorgeous peacocks and cotton roses continue to be a daily source of joy for Mr Morita.

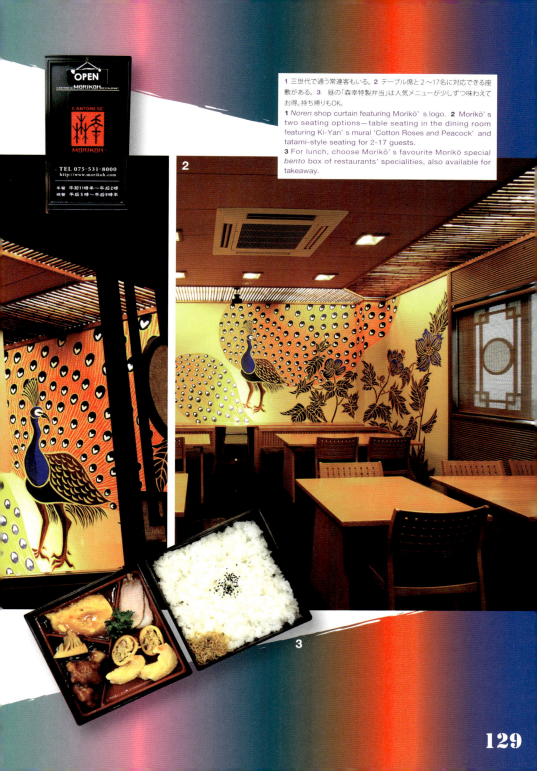

1 三世代で通う常連客もいる。 2 テーブル席と 2〜17名に対応できる座敷がある。 3 昼の「森幸特製弁当」は人気メニューが少しずつ味わえてお得。持ち帰りもOK。

1 *Noren* shop curtain featuring Morikō's logo. 2 Morikō's two seating options—table seating in the dining room featuring Ki-Yan's mural 'Cotton Roses and Peacock' and tatami-style seating for 2-17 guests.
3 For lunch, choose Morikō's favourite Morikō special *bento* box of restaurants' specialities, also available for takeaway.

1 店の前はドラマや映画によく登場する白川。春から夏は青々とした柳が美しい。**2** 京都の人だけでなく他府県からも食べにくる、昔ながらの中華の味が人気。**3** 美の象徴・芙蓉もKi-Yanが描くとクール！

1 The restaurant is located near the willow-tree lined Shirakawa River—a famous location for films and TV dramas. **2** As Morikō is one of the oldest Chinese restaurants in Kyoto, it attracts not only locals but tourists as well. **3** Ki-Yan's cotton rose.

MORIKO

map p165 - ⑦

京都市東山区白川筋
知恩院橋上ル西側 556

075-531-8000

11:30 ~13:30
17:00 ~21:00

closed Wednesday
祝日は営業

5 min walk from Higashiyama Station, Tōzai subway line

www.morikoh.com

7 KOTOWA 京都八坂

Mukuge, Red & White

Carp is dragon in heaven

11 JUROKUDAI GONDAYU
十六代権太夫

Un-Kin

慶事・吉祥のシンボルとして、お祝い事の景物に使われることが多い松竹梅。依頼を受けてもあえて描かず、「それぞれを単体で描くことはあっても、3つ揃えた絵にするのはなんとなく嫌だった」というKi-Yanが満を持して描いたのが、うどん・蕎麦の店「十六代権太夫」の壁画です。自家製麺と厳選した素材にこだわったお出汁が奏でるハーモニーに、2014年のオープン早々から大盛況。1階は初の松竹梅、2階には琳派のシンボル・雲錦の絵があり、訪れる人のお腹も心も満腹にしています。

A popular decorative motif in traditional Japanese art, *shō chiku bai* (literally 'pine, bamboo, plum') is a symbol of luck and the bringing of good fortune. Initially Ki-Yan intentionally avoided using these three typical motifs in his artwork, but he eventually decided to paint 'Shō Chiku Bai' for the *udon* and *soba* noodle restaurant Jūrokudai Gondayu. Thanks to homemade noodles and carefully selected ingredients for its original *dashi* broth, this restaurant has been flourishing since its opening in 2014. You can see the 'Shō Chiku Bai' mural on the first floor, while the second floor features 'Un-Kin' (*sakura* cherry blossoms and Japanese maple leaves)—motifs often used by Rimpa artists.

1 京都にきたら食べたい「にしんそば」。**2**「親子丼＋冷かけそば（満腹セット）」で大満足！ **3** 花見気分で食べられる２階席。

1 *Nishin soba* (herring over buckwheat noodles)—a traditional Kyoto dish. **2** *Oyako-don* (chicken and egg rice bowl) and *hiyashi-kakesoba* (cold buckwheat noodles with *tsuyu* broth) set menu. **3** Take a seat near Ki-Yan's *sakura* cherry blossom mural and feel like you are outside during *hanami* season!

1 宝ヶ池にある黒松。**2** 妙満寺の竹林の竹。**3** 北野天満宮の梅。"松竹梅"のセットは避けてきたがそれぞれは各所で描かれてきた。**4** こだわりのダシが楽しめる「きつねうどん」

1 For 'Shō Chiku Bai' Ki-Yan made sketches in three different locations around Kyoto. *Kuromatsu* (black pine) from Takaragaike. **2** Bamboo from Myōmanji Temple. **3** *Ume* (plum blossom) from Kitano Tenman-gū Shrine. **4** *Kitsune udon* (a soup of *udon* noodles and fried tofu) with homemade *dashi* broth.

JUROKUDAI GONDAYU

map p166 - ㉑

京都市東山区東大路
五条上る遊行前町 55

075-525-2005

11:00 ~16:00
11:00 ~17:00 Sat & Sun
無休

5 min walk from Kiyomizu-Gojō Station, Hankyū line

12 THE AGLIO GARDEN
アーリオガーデン

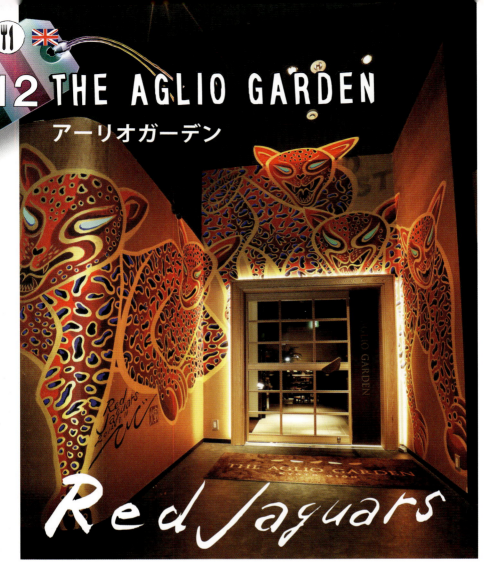

入口には赤いジャガー、店内のオリエンタルなムードのなかにはゾウ、トラ、ゴリラが集う大空間。祇園会館の4階にあり、驚くほどの広さが人気の「THE AGLIO GARDEN」は、地中海料理をベースに肉料理、タパス、アヒージョ、ピッツァなどが自慢の創作ダイニングです。店内にステージやカウンター席があるのは、かつてライブハウスだった頃の名残。ブライダルやパーティーの会場としても好評です。

Situated on the fourth floor of the movie theatre Gion Kaikan, THE AGLIO GARDEN welcomes its guests with Ki-Yan's impressive 'Red Jaguars' mural at the entrance, and an interior featuring the 'Red Tiger', 'Flying Elephants' and 'Gorillas at the Table'. This surprisingly spacious restaurant offers Mediterranean based inventive dining options, including popular dishes like tapas, ajillo and pizza. Its stage and bar counter seating—remaining from when the restaurant was used as a live house—also make it a perfect venue for parties and wedding receptions.

1 ビールやワインにぴったり！ ガーリックトースト。**2** もっちりパスタのサーモンとしめじのクリームソース リングイネ。**3** ピザの王道マルゲリータ。**4** 京豆腐一筋「とようけ屋 山本」の豆腐を使ったサラダ。**5** 抹茶シフォンケーキ＆辻利抹茶アイス。

1 Start your dinner with garlic bread matched with a glass of wine or beer! **2** Linguine with salmon and creamy *shimeji* mushroom sauce. **3** The margherita pizza—always a good choice! **4** Tofu salad with homemade tofu from Toyoukeya Yamamoto—a local tofu shop with an over 100-year history. **5** For dessert try the *matcha* chiffon cake topped with Tsujiri-brand *matcha* ice-cream.

THE AGLIO GARDEN

map p165 -⑳

京都市東山区祇園町
北側 323 祇園会館 4F

075-533-8989

17:00 ~ 23:00 Sun - Thu
17:00 ~ 24:00 Fri - Sat
無休

10 min walk from Higashiyama Station, Tōzai subway line or Gion-Shijō Station, Keihan line

www.k-company.net/agliogarden

map p165 - 18

COLUMN 3
JAPANESE FENG SHUI
方位学

壁画は額に入ったタブローとは違い、その空間に描かれた入れ墨と同じ。消すことも移動させることもできない。壁画を依頼してくる人は、それを覚悟の上でないと私は描かない。建築家やコーディネーターなどから話があっても、必ずオーナーと会って、そのことを確認してから依頼を受ける。もしオーナーが知らなかったら、壁画は落書きとなるからだ。

私は構図を決めるのに「方位」を重視している。方位や風水を勉強したわけではないが、自然と共に生きてきた私たちにとって、その空間の光と風を素直に取り入れたいと考えるようになった。東と南の辰巳の方向、または西と北の戌亥の方位を軸に構図を考える。そこの方角に絵を向かわせるか、その方位から光や風を感じるか。その流れを大切にして壁画を描くことにしている。

A mural painting is different from a framed painting; it resembles a tattoo. Nobody can erase or move it. Therefore, I am only ready to paint if the client is prepared for this. Even if I am asked to paint by an architect or coordinator, I definitely have to meet the owner and confirm his or her intention before I begin my work. Otherwise my work might end up as illegal graffiti.

When I plan mural paintings, I always attach importance to the *hōi* – the geomancy of the space. This is not because I have studied Feng Shui, but I have gradually become interested in how to incorporate the light and wind patterns of a particular space into my mural paintings. I always plan my composition around the South-East axis, which is *tatsumi* (dragon and snake), and North-West axis, which is *inui* (dog and boar). Before I start painting, I consider whether I should paint the motifs toward one direction, or to take into consideration the light and wind patterns from that direction. I take these concepts of flow very seriously when producing my work.

SOU・SOU

Ki-Yan Stuzio (FLYING HIDEKI PROJECT) × SOU・SOU

SHOP 1 COLLABORATION

地下足袋 "がんじがらめ"
Jika-Tabi – 'Ganjigarame'

日本人がふだん何気なしに使う相づち言葉「そう、そう」から生まれた「SOU・SOU」。オリジナルのテキスタイルで、地下足袋をはじめとするSOU・SOU流の和装や雑貨など、新しい日本のライフスタイルを提案する京都発のブランドです。Ki-Yanとのコラボでカッコいい地下足袋や現代的な和装、テキスタイルなどがたくさん誕生しています。

collaboration
棟梁地下足袋 10枚小鉤 "Flying Elephants"
Tōryō-Jika-Tabi – 'Flying Elephants' with ten kohaze clasps.

collaboration
Ki-Yanの祇園祭絵図
'Gion Festival'

2階には「ほそつじいへえ TEAHOUSE supported by MLESNA」。
EIRAKUYA's Hosotsuji Ihee Tea House on the second floor of the shop's Gion branch.

1615年に呉服商として創業した「永楽屋 細辻伊兵衛商店」は、2015年で創立400年を迎える手ぬぐい専門店です。明治初期から昭和初期にかけて製造されていた手ぬぐいを型友禅で復刻するほか、Ki-Yanなど様々なアーティストとのコラボも展開。実用性の高い手ぬぐいですが、タペストリー風に壁に飾ったり額装してみたりと、アート感覚あふれるインテリアとしても楽しみたいものばかりです。

Celebrating its 400th year of business in 2015, EIRAKUYA is a *tenugui* (thin cotton Japanese hand towel) shop originally founded as a fabric shop for kimonos in 1615. Today EIRAKUYA has been reproducing vintage *tenugui* designs from the early 20th century using the *kata-yūzen* technique (a traditional paper pattern dying technique from Kyoto). The shop also collaborates with many artists, including Ki-Yan. While *tenugui* are practical, everyday use items in Japanese culture, EIRAKUYA's *tenugui* are so beautiful that they are also treated as decorative items to be framed and displayed as art.

永楽屋十四世・細辻伊兵衛氏の似顔絵。
An illustration of Hosotsuji Ihee, the 14th generation owner of EIRAKUYA

EIRAKUYA

map p165 - ⑯

京都市東山区四条通
大和大路東入ル祇園町
北側 242

075-532-1125

10:30 ~ 22:00
無休

3 min walk from Gion Shijō Station, Keihan line or 5 min walk from Kawaramachi Station, Hankyū line

www.eirakuya.jp

SHOP 4 COLLABORATION

KOMARUYA SUMII 小丸屋 住井

Ki-Yan Stuzio FLYING HIDEKI PROJECT × KOMARUYA

「うちわは相手のために心地よい涼風をほどよくあおいであげる、日本人のもてなしの心を伝える道具です」と話すのは「小丸屋 住井」の十代女将・住井啓子さん。うちわの元祖といわれる深草うちわを復元し、花街の舞妓芸妓の名前を入れた京丸うちわの発祥の店としても知られます。Ki-Yanとのコラボで作られた鯉の飾りうちわも、見る人を元気にしてくれるもてなしグッズです。

新深草うちわ
Shin-fukakusa uchiwa

'The uchiwa (round fan) is a traditional Japanese tool which expresses hospitality by sending a refreshing breeze during Japan's hot summers', explains Keiko Sumii, the tenth-generation member of the Sumii family to own the uchiwa fan shop KOMARUYA SUMII. The store is famous for kyōmaru uchiwa (fans with imprinted names of geiko [geisha] and maiko on the back) and shin-fukakusa uchiwa, a reproduction of the prototype fukakusa uchiwa (a fan popular in the Edo period made from bamboo grown in Fukakusa, Kyoto). Both of these fan designs originated from the ancestors of KOMARUYA. The modern uchiwa made in collaboration with Ki-Yan is a round fan featuring the 'Carp is Dragon in Heaven' motif.

You'll love the reverse side of the uchiwa we designed with Ki-Yan ... It's red!!

Ki-Yanコラボうちわの裏は驚きの真っ赤!

collaboration
鯉 飾りうちわ
'Carp is Dragon in Heaven' uchiwa

KOMARUYA
map p167 - ④
京都市左京区岡崎
円勝寺町 91-54
075-771-2229
10:00 ~ 18:00
closed Sunday

5 min walk from Higashiyama Station, Tōzai subway line

http://komaruya.kyoto.jp

BAISEN-AN

collaboration

青蓮院を思わせる"生命賛歌"
'Paean of Life' (motif from Shōren-in Temple)

踊りに使われる扇子は華やか
Folding fan for traditional Japanese dance

Founded in 1823, MIYAWAKI BAISEN-AN is a traditional kyō-machiya (Kyoto townhouse) folding fan shop that features distinctive elements of traditional Japanese architecture and interior design including a *mushikomado* (clay lattice window), *bengaragoshi* (vermillion coloured wooden latticework) and *haridashi-no shōgi* (folding bench). The shop offers a wide selection of *sensu* (folding fans) ranging from practical fans for surviving Japan's humid summer, to *maisen* (folding fans for traditional dancing). In addition to traditional fans, MIYAWAKI BAISEN-AN works in collaboration with Ki-Yan to produce a line of quality modern fans designed with bold, vivid colours and the artist's signature motifs.

平安時代を彷彿とさせる檜扇。
Heian period-style folding fan made of *hinoki* wood (Japanese cypress)

投扇興の道具。扇子を使った
日本の伝統的な遊び
Tōsenkyō - Japanese traditional fan-tossing game set

MIYAWAKI BAISEN-AN

map p164 - ⑤
京都市中京区六角通
富小路東入ル大黒町 80-3

075-221-0181

9:00 ~ 18:00
in summer ~ 19:00
無休（年末年始除く）

10 min walk from Kawara-machi Station, Hankyū line

www.baisenan.co.jp

EPILOGUE
あとがき

突然、マルタ・ヴァヴジニャク・イヂチさんというポーランドの女性がKi-Yan StuzioをStuzioを訪ねてきた。『魅惑の東欧・ポーランド　インテリア＆雑貨めぐり』というＡ５判のガイドブックを挨拶がわりにいただいた。

その単行本は私の大学（京都市立芸術大学）の恩師リチ・上野＝リックス教授を思い出させる、東欧の匂いに溢れていた。リチ教授はオーストリアのウィーン出身だったが、アメリカ的なコマーシャルではなく、東欧に残っていたプロパガンダ的な感覚、単なる商業主義に翻弄されず、人間の本質、温かさを忘れていない社会派的デザインを求める教育者だった。

商業デザイン科の教授だった彼女のカリキュラムは切り紙、貼り絵、木工、金工、竹工、ガラス絵などカテゴリーにこだわらない自由なものだった。私が壁画を描くに至るのは、日生劇場のレストラン・アクトレスの彼女の壁画制作を手伝ったことが原点になっている。

マルタさんの仕事は忘れかけている人間のあったかさと切り抜き、吹き出しなど現代的感覚のポップな手法も取り入れ、カッコよかった。彼女に私が描いた壁画の飲食店のガイドブックのデザイン編集を何の躊躇もなく依頼する。

後に知るのだが、一柳慧さん（作曲家・ピアニスト）の正倉院の楽器を復元した現代音楽のヨーロッパ・ツアーを、パウロ教皇の出身地ポーランドのクラクフからスタートするプロジェクトの通訳を担当したのがマルタさんで、当時のプロデューサーは私が若い頃お世話になった制作会社ＡＡＰの社長・浅井栄一さんだった。巡り廻った、国境を超えた縁を感じている。

　　　　　　　　　　木村 英輝・Ki-Yan

One day a lady from Poland, Marta Wawrzyniak-Ijichi, suddenly visited my studio and gave me her book as a gift—a guidebook introducing Polish products and interior design to a Japanese audience.

With its Eastern European touch, this book reminded me of my former Kyoto City University of Arts teacher, Austrian-born Felice "Lizzi" Ueno-Rix. Lizzi was a commercial design course lecturer who was not following American commercialism. Instead she tried to convey the idea of social awareness in design that reflects warmth and human nature, an element found in propaganda-influenced designs of Eastern Europe. Her course spanned various subjects such as paper art, collage, bamboo, wood, metal and glasswork. In fact, the origin of my mural artwork comes from my experience in assisting Lizzi in painting a mural at the Actress restaurant in Tokyo's Nissay Theatre.

I liked Marta's design work, which expressed a type of human warmth that we often tend to forget, while at the same time having a contemporary and pop touch through the use of cut-outs and speech bubbles. So with no hesitation, I asked her to design the guidebook to my murals in Kyoto.

I later realised that Marta worked as an interpreter and coordinator for a concert tournée in Europe in which contemporary music composed by Toshi Ichiyanagi was played on ancient reconstructed musical instruments from the Shōsōin Imperial Treasure House. The tournée debuted in Kraków, Poland—the birthplace of Pope John Paul II. The producer of this international event was Eiichi Asai, the general producer at AAP Co., Ltd, whom I have known since I was young and to whom I owe much gratitude. I feel this strange coincidence must be the hand of fate.

INFO & MAPS

P.22
ゼスト御池 Zest

京都の繁華街・河原町御池にある地下街。書店や飲食店など約40もの店が揃う。

An underground shopping area in downtown Kyoto, Kawaramachi-Oike. You will find around 40 stores here, including bookstores and restaurants.

MAP P.165 - ❷
京都市中京区御池通寺町東入下本能寺前町492-1
☎ 075-253-3100（ゼスト御池事務局）
HOURS　物販 Retail Store　　10:30〜20:00
　　　　飲食 Restaurant　　11:00〜21:30
ACCESS　地下鉄東西線「京都市役所前」すぐ
　　　　0 min walk from Kyoto Shiyakusho-mae Station, Tōzai subway line

P.28
MKボウル 上賀茂 MK Bowl

フットサル・カラオケ・バイキングレストランなども併設されたボウリング場。

A bowling alley with a futsal area, karaoke and a buffet restaurant.

MAP P.166 - ㉒
京都市北区上賀茂西河原町1-1
☎ 075-701-2131
HOURS　月〜木 10:00〜26:00
　　　　金土祝前日 10:00〜27:00
　　　　日祝 8:00〜26:00
ACCESS　市バス1・37番系統「西賀茂車庫前」徒歩10分
　　　　10 min walk from Nishikamo shako-mae bus stop, bus 1 or 37

P.36
京都市動物園 Kyoto City Zoo

明治36年、日本で2番目に開園した動物園。Ki-Yanの壁画は類人猿舎で見られる。

Japan's second zoo, which opened in 1903. Ki-Yan's mural can be found in the great ape house.

MAP P.167 - ❶
京都市左京区岡崎法勝寺町　岡崎公園内
☎ 075-771-0210
HOURS　3〜11月 9:00〜17:00
　　　　12〜2月 9:00〜16:30
ACCESS　地下鉄東西線「東山」「蹴上」徒歩10分
　　　　10 min walk from Higashiyama Station or Keage Station, Tōzai subway line

P.38
香東園やましな Kōtōen Yamashina

特別養護老人ホーム、ケアハウスなど種々な施設を整備する居宅介護施設。

A home care centre equipped with various facilities including a special nursing home and a nursing care centre.

MAP P.166 - ㉘
京都市山科区西野野色町15-88
☎ 075-595-6511
ACCESS　地下鉄東西線「御陵」徒歩15分
　　　　15 min walk from Misasagi Station, Tōzai subway line

P.42
青蓮院門跡 Shōren-in Temple

天台宗の京都五ケ室門跡の一つで日本三不動の一つである青不動明王（国宝）を有する。

One of the five Monzeki temples of the Tendai sect in Kyoto. It houses the Blue Fudo-Myoo (a national treasure), one of the three fudos of Japan.

MAP P.167 - ❺
京都市東山区粟田口三条坊町69-1
☎ 075-561-2345
HOURS　9:00〜17:00
ACCESS　地下鉄東西線「東山」下車徒歩5分
　　　　5 min walk from Higashiyama Station, Tōzai subway line

P.46
タキイ種苗株式会社 Takii

野菜、花の種苗から農園芸資材まで幅広く開発・販売をおこなう。
A company involved in the development and sale of an extensive range of products ranging from vegetables and flower seeds, to agricultural and horticultural materials.

> **MAP P.167 - ⑧**
> 京都市下京区梅小路通猪熊東入南夷町180
> ☎ 075-365-0123
> HOURS 9:00～17:40
> ※見学不可　Sightseeing not allowed

P.58
クレヴィア京都 四条後院通
CREVIA

伊藤忠都市開発による新築分譲マンション。
A new apartment complex constructed as part of an Itochu urban development project.

> **MAP P.166 - ⑯**
> 京都市中京区壬生坊城町5番8
> ※見学不可　Sightseeing not allowed

P.74
レストラン ヴィトラ
Restaurant VITRA

北山ル・アンジェ教会に併設する創作フレンチレストラン。ウエディングパーティーの会場として大人気。
A creative French restaurant and famous wedding reception venue built in the KITAYAMA Chapelle Des Anges.

> **MAP P.166 - ㉓**
> 京都市左京区松ヶ崎井出ヶ海道町1-7
> ☎ 075-706-7676
> HOURS 17:30～22:30　火曜定休、完全予約制
> 　　　 closed Tuesday, by appointment only
> ACCESS 地下鉄烏丸線「松ヶ崎」徒歩すぐ
> 　　　 0 min walk from Matsuga-saki Station, Karasuma subway line

P.102
京都府警 中京警察署
Nakagyō Police Station

京都府警が管轄する警察署の一つ。Ki-Yanの壁画は玄関を入ってすぐにある。
A Kyoto police station. Ki-Yan's mural is near the entrance.

> **MAP P.166 - ⑮**
> 京都市中京区壬生坊城町48-16
> ☎ 075-823-0110
> ACCESS 阪急京都線「大宮」徒歩5分
> 　　　 5 min walk from Ōmiya Station, Hankyū Kyoto line

P.112
独立行政法人国立病院機構　京都医療センター
Kyoto Medical Center

39診療科を標榜している、高度総合医療施設として医療活動を行う国立の高度総合医療施設。
A highly advanced public medical facility with 39 medical departments.

> **MAP P.166 - ㉙**
> 京都市伏見区深草向畑町1-1
> ☎ 075-641-9161
> ACCESS 京阪本線「藤森」徒歩8分
> 　　　 8 min walk from Fujinomori Station, Keihan line

P.120
WAZAGU 京都国際工芸センター

京都をはじめとする日本の伝統工芸品の販売や、需要開拓などをおこなう。館内にはセレクトショップも。
A Kyoto centre that sells and develops new markets for Japanese traditional crafts. There is also a select shop inside.

> **MAP P.164 - ③**
> 京都市中京区高倉通三条下ル
> ☎ 075-223-5353
> HOURS 10:00～18:00
> ACCESS 地下鉄烏丸線・東西線「烏丸御池」徒歩5分
> 　　　 5 min walk from Karasuma-oike Station, Karasuma or Tōzai subway line

P.126
京都タカシマヤ Takashimaya

1831年創業の百貨店。ライブペイントなどのイベントや展示会、カタログなどKi-Yanとのコラボは多数。

A department store, which opened in 1831. The store often collaborates with Ki-Yan through live painting events, exhibitions and catalogs.

> **MAP P.165 - ㉔**
> 京都市下京区四条通河原町西入真町52番地
> ☎ 075-221-8811
> HOURS 10:00〜20:00
> ACCESS 阪急京都線「河原町」すぐ、京阪「祇園四条」徒歩5分
> 0 min walk from Kawaramachi Station, Hankyū Kyoto line
> 5 min walk from Gion-shijō Station, Keihan line

P.132
KOTOWA 京都八坂

結婚式場。「美しく、新しい結婚式」がコンセプト。

A wedding hall built around the concept of a 'new and beautiful wedding'

> **MAP P.165 - ⑲**
> 京都市東山区祇園町北側310
> ☎ 075-551-4122
> HOURS 平日 weekdays 12:00〜20:00
> 土日祝 weekend 10:00〜20:00
> 火・水定休 closed Tuesday and Wednesday
> ACCESS 京阪本線「祇園四条」徒歩5分、阪急京都線「河原町」徒歩8分
> 5 min walk from Gion-shijō Station, Keihan line
> 8 min walk from Kawaramachi Station, Hankyū Kyoto line

P.134
祇園倭美坐 GION WABIZA

「ものづくり京都」を体験できる、新しい商業施設。

Fine traditional crafts, including reasonably priced dolls, ceramics, lacquerware, textiles, and bonsai, can be found here.

> **MAP P.165 - ⑰**
> 京都市東山区祇園町北側275
> ☎ 075-541-1196
> HOURS 10:00〜19:00
> ACCESS 京阪本線「祇園四条」徒歩5分、阪急京都線「河原町」徒歩10分
> 5 min walk from Gion-shijō Station, Keihan line
> 10 min walk from Kawaramachi Station, Hankyū Kyoto line

P.136
駒屋 花れ家 Bar HANARE

宮川町のお茶屋「駒屋」の離れとして、花街の風情とワインやカクテルを楽しめるワインバー。

A wine bar, which is an annex of the "Komaya" teahouse in Miyagawa-chō. Here one can get a feel for the geisha district while enjoying wine and cocktails.

> **MAP P.165 - ㉗**
> 京都市東山区宮川筋3-282
> ☎ 075-525-5588
> HOURS 19:00〜25:00 日曜定休 closed Sunday
> ACCESS 京阪「祇園四条」徒歩5分
> 5 min walk from Gion-shijo Station, Keihan line

P.138
株式会社タナックス TANA-X

店頭広告をはじめとしたセールスプロモーションと、包装資材を事業の柱とする企業。

A company that started its business with sales promotions and selling packing materials.

> **MAP P.164 - ㉙**
> 京都市下京区五条通烏丸東入松屋町438
> ☎ 075-361-2000
> ※見学不可 Sightseeing not allowed

P.146
祇園大茶會 Daichakai

祇園商店街振興組合主催による、八坂神社・円山公園で開催される特別なおもてなしの呈茶席。

A tea ceremony event that places special importance on hospitality. Held at the Yasaka Shrine, Maruyama Park and organized by the Gion Shopping Street Promotion Associates.

> **MAP P.165 - ⑱**
> 主催 八坂神社参道 祇園商店街振興組合
> ☎ 075-531-2288

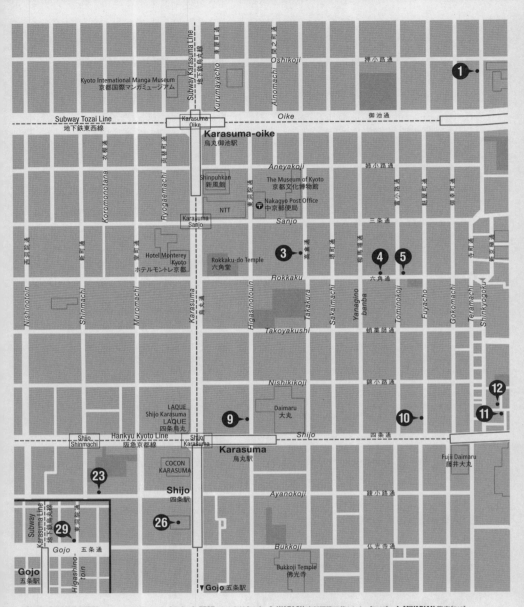

1. NOUVELLE VAGUE KYOTO ヌーベルバーグKYOTO [P80] 2. ZEST ゼスト御池 [P22] 3. WAZAGU 京都国際工芸センター [P120] 4. MIYABIAN 雅庵 [P18]
5. MIYAWAKI BAISEN-AN 宮脇賣扇庵 [P158] 6. ICHIZAWA SHINZABURO HANPU 一澤信三郎帆布 [P152] 7. MORIKO ぎをん森幸 [P128]
8. TOKU 和牛焼肉 德 [P92] 9. KATSUKURA HIGASHINOTOIN かつくら 四条東洞院店 [P76] 10. GONTARO 京都権太呂 本店 [P32]
11. SOU・SOU ZAIFU SOU・SOU 在釜 [P40] 12. SOU・SOU SOU・SOU [P150] 13. HYAKUREN 百練 [P10] 14. TAISUSHI 江戸前にぎり鯛寿司 [P110]
15. TEMPURA KITAMURA 天麩羅きたむら [P8] 16. EIRAKUYA 永楽屋細辻伊兵衛商店 祇園店 [P154] 17. GION WABIZA 祇園倭美坐 [P134]
18. DAICHAKAI 祇園大茶會 [P146] 19. KOTOWA KOTOWA 京都八坂 [P132] 20. THE AGLIO GARDEN アーリオ・ガーデン [P144]
21. KI-YAN STUZIO Ki-Yan Stuzio 祇園本店 [P60] 22. KI-YAN STUZIO Ki-Yan Stuzio 祇園石段下店 [P60] 23. GOH-NO TORA 五黄の寅 [P54]
24. TAKASHIMAYA 京都タカシマヤ [P126] 25. CHORAKUKAN 長楽館 コーラル [P88] 26. TOH-LEE からすま京都ホテル 中国料理 桃李 [P106]
27. BAR HANARE 駒屋 花れ家 [P136] 28. WABIYA KOREKIDO 侘家古暦堂 祇園花見小路本店 [P72] 29. TANA-X 株式会社タナックス [P138]

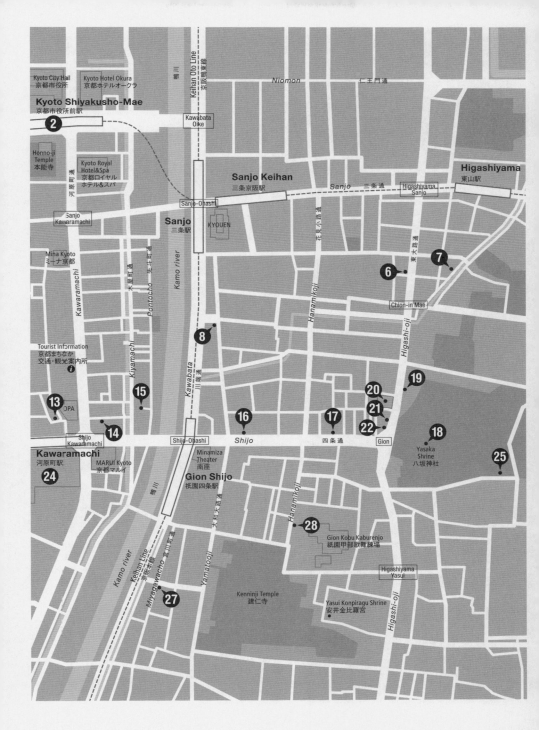

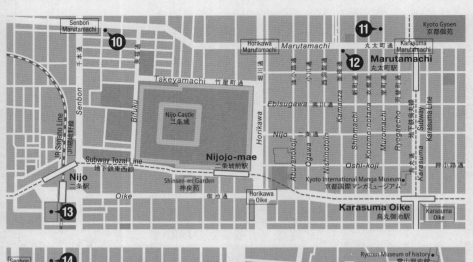
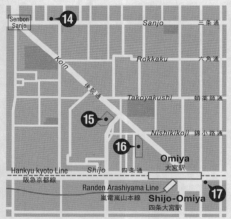
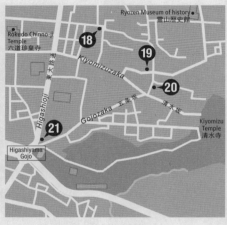

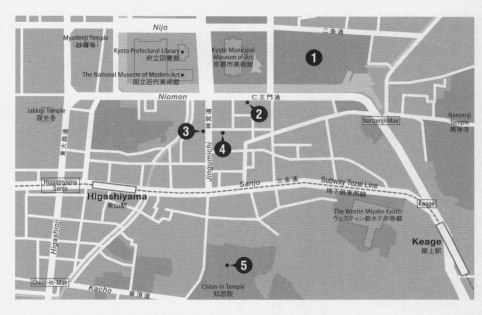
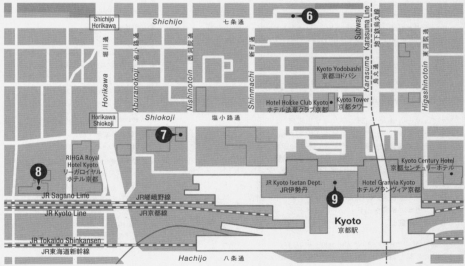

1. KYOTO CITY ZOO 京都市動物園 [P36]　2. KYOTO TRAVELERS INN 京都トラベラーズ・イン [P118]　3. HOURANDOU HEIAN-JINGU 峯嵐堂 平安神宮店 [P16]
4. KOMARUYA SUMII 小丸屋 住井 [P156]　5. SHOREN-IN TEMPLE 青蓮院門跡 [P42]　6. WINE KURA SHIORI Wine 蔵しおり [P24]
7. KYOTO HATOYA 京湯元 ハトヤ瑞鳳閣 [P94]　8. TAKII タキイ種苗株式会社 [P46]　9. KATSUKURA KYOTO STATION かつくら 京都駅ビルThe Cube店 [P62]
10. ADACHI 京の惣菜 あだち [P98]　11. CHIRIRI 京都つゆしゃぶ CHIRIRI [P68]　12. HAMAMURA 京都中華 ハマムラ [P12]
13. TAKABASHI RAMEN たかばしラーメン BiVi二条店 [P56]　14. PIITO 匹十 [P86]　15. NAKAGYO POLICE STATION 京都府警 中京警察署 [P102]
16. CREVIA クレヴィア京都四条後院通 [P58]　17. YAOISO フルーツパーラーヤオイソ [P44]　18. HOURANDOU YASAKA 峯嵐堂 八坂店 [P14]
19. YUME KOBO KYO 夢工房 京 三年坂店 [P104]　20. YAMASHITA 京・お漬物処 やました [P70]　21. JUROKUDAI GONDAYU 十六代権太夫 [P140]
22. MK BOWL MKボウル 上賀茂 [P28]　23. RESTAURANT VITRA レストラン ヴィトラ [P74]　24. DOYANEN どやねん [P116]　25. GYU OTA 牛 おおた [P20]
26. EX CAFE eX cafe 嵐山本店 [P122]　27. NOUVELLE VAGUE KYOTO LA VILLAGE ヌーベルバーグ KYOTO ラ・ヴィラージュ [P80]
28. KOTOEN YAMASHINA 香東園やましな [P38]　29. KYOTO MEDICAL CENTER 京都医療センター [P112]

木村英輝
Hideki Kimura (Ki-Yan)

絵師。1942年大阪府生まれ。京都市立美術大学（現・市立芸術大学）図案科卒業。同大講師を務める。
日本のロック黎明期に、日本初のロックフェスの開催、村八分のオーガナイザー、内田裕也とのワールド・ロックフェスなど数々のプロデュースを成し遂げ、伝説を残す。
還暦より絵師に。究極のアマチュアリズムを標榜し、「『ライブ』な街に絵を描きたい」と手がけた壁画は国内外で150カ所を超える。作品集に『生きる儘』『無我夢中』『LIVE』など。

木村英輝オフィシャルWebサイト：www.ki-yan.com

Born in Osaka in 1942, painter Hideki Kimura (Ki-Yan) graduated with a degree in design from the Kyoto City University of Arts. Upon graduation, Ki-Yan first worked as a lecturer at his alma mater, then as a rock music producer. As an ambassador of rock and roll in Japan's early days of rock music, he produced the Japanese rock band Murahachibu, co-produced the world rock concert with Yūya Uchida, and organized many other legendary events, including Japan's first rock festival. Ki-Yan began his work as a mural artist at the age of sixty. Pursuing a form of ultimate amateurism he has already painted more than 150 murals around Japan and abroad. His books include 'Ikiru Mama', 'Muga Muchū' and 'Live'.

マルタ・ヴァヴジニャク・イヂチ
Marta Wawrzyniak-Ijichi

デザイナー、通訳/翻訳。ブルガリア生まれ、ポーランド・クラクフ育ち。ポーランドで日本学科を卒業、ドイツで東洋美術史を学んだ後、来日。ポーランド語、日本語、英語、ドイツ語、ブルガリア語の通訳/翻訳として活躍。東京でインテリアデザインを学び、2011年『魅惑の東欧・ポーランド インテリア＆雑貨めぐり』を出版。取材、写真、デザイン、原稿のすべてを担当。Ki-Yanのユニークなアートに出会い、バイリンガルの本書を通じもう一つのクールジャパンの文化として世界に紹介。

Bulgarian born designer and translator, raised in Kraków, Poland. Marta has a degree in Japanese Studies from Jagiellonian University in Kraków and studied East Asian art history in Germany before moving to Japan. Fluent in five languages: Polish, Japanese, English, German and Bulgarian. After completing studies in Interior Design in Tokyo, she published—as author, photographer and designer—her first book in Japanese, a guidebook to Polish products and interior design. Recently she discovered Ki-Yan's unique mural art and through this book is introducing to you his 'cool' take on Japanese culture.

取材・執筆　林里嘉子
Interview & Writing by Rikako Hayashi

写真　打田浩一
Photography by Koichi Uchida

本文デザイン・英訳
マルタ・ヴァヴジニャク・イヂチ
Book design & Translation/English adaptation by Marta Wawrzyniak-Ijichi

装丁デザイン　いわながさとこ
Cover design by Satoko Iwanaga

地図デザイン　齋藤直己
Map design by Naomi Saito

印刷・製本　泰和印刷株式会社
Printed by Taiwa Print co.,Ltd.

一部写真提供　伊地知直緒人、株式会社エレファントスタッフ
Photography by Naoto Ijichi on pp. 5, 15, 40, 41, 44, 49, 63, 90, 122 and photos courtesy of Elephant Co., Ltd.

Special thanks to: Karly Burch, Rosemary Hanly, Fred Fink, Pip Vice and Brigitte Staples.

英文での表現と本全体の統一感を重視して翻訳しています。幾つかの箇所で対訳となっていない部分があります。

The English translation of the original Japanese text has been adjusted stylistically for the whole publication. In some passages the translation is not literal.

本書は、外国人の方を意識したデータ構成です。

外国人が見つけた
KYOTO グルメ＆アート
Ki-Yan ギャラリーをめぐる

Ki-Yan's KYOTO Food & Art
Explore Kyoto through
the Artwork of a Japanese Pop Artist

2015年11月2日　初版第一刷発行

著　者	Marta & Ki-Yan
発行者	三島邦弘
発行所	（株）ミシマ社 〒152-0035 東京都目黒区自由が丘2-6-13 TEL 03-3724-5616 FAX 03-3724-5618 e-mail　hatena@mishimasha.com URL　http://www.mishimasha.com/
振　替	00160-1-372976
制　作	（株）ミシマ社 京都オフィス

ⓒ2015 Marta & Ki-Yan Printed in JAPAN
ISBN：978-4-903908-68-7
本書の無断複写・複製・転載を禁じます。